Limited Classical Reprint Library

THE

EPISTLE TO THE HEBREWS

BY

THOMAS CHARLES EDWARDS, D.D.

Foreword by
Dr. Cyril J. Barber

Klock & Klock Christian Publishers, Inc.
2527 Girard Avenue North
Minneapolis, Minnesota 55411

Originally published by
Hodder & Stoughton
London, 1911

ISBN: 0-86524-154-6

Printed by Klock & Klock in the U.S.A.
1982 Reprint

FOREWORD

The mark of a true scholar lies in his ability to explain profound truths in simple terms. Such a person stimulates us. He infuses in us a desire for knowledge, develops our capacity for discernment, and sends us on a quest which continuously involves relating the truth we have learned to life.

Such a man was Thomas Charles Edwards (1837-1900). Educated in the universities of London (B.A.) and Oxford (M.A.) and the recipient of two doctorates in divinity, the one from the University of Edinburgh and the other from the University of Wales, Dr. Edwards possessed the ability to explain complex issues in easily understood terms. He taught for several years at Oxford before becoming the principal of the University College of Wales in Aberystwyth.

Evidence of Dr. Edwards' magisterial ability to deal with complex issues may be found in his commentary on Paul's first letter to the church at Corinth. In that work he handled the grammar and syntax with consumate skill and laid bare the Apostle's thought as no other commentary had done. It is no wonder that his study of this portion of God's Word has been one of the most eagerly sought after of all exegetical works on First Corinthians.

In like manner in the commentary now before the reader--a commentary written for lay people--Dr. Edwards has explained the theme of the letter to the Hebrews in such a way as to reveal the masterful development of the biblical writer's purpose. Readers cannot fail to be blessed by Thomas Edwards' clear, convincing presentation of the all-sufficiency and superiority of Christ.

We are grateful that so excellent a work has been selected for reprinting.

Cyril J. Barber
Author, *The Minister's Library*

PREFACE.

IN this volume the sole aim of the writer has been to trace the unity of thought in one of the greatest and most difficult books of the New Testament. He has endeavoured to picture his reader as a member of what is known in the Sunday-schools of Wales as "the teachers' class," a thoughtful Christian layman, who has no Greek, and desires only to be assisted in his efforts to come at the real bearing and force of words and to understand the connection of the sacred author's ideas. It may not be unnecessary to add that this design by no means implies less labour or thought on the part of the writer. But it does imply that the labour is veiled. Criticism is rigidly excluded.

The writer has purposely refrained from discussing the question of the authorship of the Epistle, simply because he has no new light to throw on this standing enigma of the Church. He is convinced that St. Paul is neither the actual author nor the originator of the treatise.

In case theological students may wish to consult the volume when they study the Epistle to the Hebrews, they will find the Greek given at the foot of the page, to serve as a catch-word, whenever any point of criticism or of interpretation seems to the writer to deserve their attention.

T. C. E.

ABERYSTWYTH, *April* 12*th*, 1888.

CONTENTS.

SUMMARY.

I. THE REVELATION IN A SON: i. 1-3.

1. The previous revelation was in portions; this in a Son, Who is the Heir and the Creator.

2. The previous revelation was in divers manners; this in a Son, Who is (1) the effulgence of God's glory; (2) the image of His substance; (3) the Sustainer of all things; (4) the eternal Priest-King.

II. THE SON AND THE ANGELS: i. 4-ii. 18.

1. The Revealer of God Son of God: i. 4-ii. 4.

2. The Son the Representative of man: ii. 5-18. (1) He is crowned with glory as Son, that His propitiation may prove effectual, and His humiliation involves a propitiatory death. (2) His glory consists in being Leader of His people, and His humiliation fitted Him for leadership. (3) His glory consists in power to consecrate men to God, and His humiliation endowed Him with this power. (4) His glory consists in the destruction of Satan, and Satan is destroyed through the Son's humiliation.

III. FUNDAMENTAL ONENESS OF THE DISPENSATIONS: iii. 1-iv. 13.

1. Moses and Christ are equally God's stewards.

2. The threatenings of God under the Old Testament are in force in reference to apostasy from Christ.

3. The promises of God are still in force.

IV. THE GREAT HIGH-PRIEST: iv. 4-v. 10.

    1. His sympathy.

    2. His authority.

V. (A DIGRESSION) THE IMPOSSIBILITY OF RENEWAL IN THE CASE OF SCOFFERS: v. 11-vi. 8.

    Their renewal is impossible (1) because the doctrine of Christianity is practical, and (2) because God's punishment of cynicism is the destruction of the spiritual faculty.

VI. (CONTINUATION OF THE DIGRESSION.) THE IMPOSSIBILITY OF FAILURE: vi. 9-20.

VII. THE ALLEGORY OF MELCHIZEDEK: vii. 1-28.

    1. Melchizedek foreshadows the kingship of Christ.

    2. Melchizedek foreshadows the personal greatness of Christ.

    3. The allegory teaches the existence of a priesthood other than that of Aaron, viz., the priesthood founded on an oath.

    4. The allegory sets forth the eternal duration of Christ's priesthood.

VIII. THE NEW COVENANT: viii. 1.

    1. A new covenant promised through Jeremiah: viii. 1-13. The new covenant would excel (1) in respect of the moral law; (2) in respect of knowledge of God; (3) in respect of forgiveness of sins.

    2. A new covenant symbolized in the tabernacle: ix. 1-14.

    3. A new covenant ratified in the death of Christ: ix. 15-x. 18.

IX. AN ADVANCE IN THE EXHORTATION: x. 19-39.

X. FAITH AN ASSURANCE AND A PROOF: xi. 1-3.

XI. THE FAITH OF ABRAHAM: xi. 8-19.

    1. His faith compared with the faith of Noah.

    2. His faith compared with the faith of Enoch.

    3. His faith compared with the faith of Abel.

" God, having of old time spoken unto the fathers in the prophets by divers portions and in divers manners, hath at the end of these days spoken unto us in His Son, Whom He appointed Heir of all things, through Whom also He made the worlds ; Who being the effulgence of His glory, and the very image of His substance, and upholding all things by the word of His power, when He had made purification of sins, sat down on the right hand of the Majesty on high."—HEB. i. 1—3 (R.V.).

CHAPTER I.

"GOD hath spoken." The eternal silence has been broken. We have a revelation. That God has spoken unto men is the ground of all religion. Theologians often distinguish between natural religion and revealed. We may fairly question if all worship is not based on some revelation of God. Prayer is the echo in man's spirit of God's own voice. Men learn to speak to the Father Who is in heaven as children come to utter words : by hearing their parent speak. It is the deaf who are also dumb. God speaks first, and prayer answers as well as asks. Men reveal themselves to the God Who has revealed Himself to them.

The Apostle is, however, silent about the revelations of God in nature and in conscience. He passes them by because we, sinful men, have lost the key to the language of creation and of our own moral nature. We know that He speaks through them, but we do not know what He says. If we were holy, it would be otherwise. All nature would be vocal, "like some sweet beguiling melody." But to us the universe is a hieroglyphic which we cannot decipher, until we discover in another revelation the key that will make all plain.

More strange than this is the Apostle's omission to speak of the Mosaic dispensation as a revelation of God. We should have expected the verse to run on this wise : " God, having spoken unto the fathers in the sacrifices and in the prophets, institutions, and inspired words," etc. But the author says nothing about rites, institutions, dispensations, and laws. The reason apparently is that he wishes to compare with the revelation in Christ the highest, purest, and fullest revelation given before ; and the most complete revelation vouchsafed to men, before the Son came to declare the Father, is to be found, not in sacrifices, but in the words of promise, not in the institutions, but in holy men, who were sent, time after time, to quicken the institutions into new life or to preach new truths. The prophets were seers and poets. Nature's highest gift is imagination, whether it " makes " a world that transcends nature or " sees " what in nature is hidden from the eyes of ordinary men. This faculty of the true poet, elevated, purified, taken possession of by God's Holy Spirit, became the best instrument of revelation, until the word of prophecy was made more sure through the still better gift of the Son.

But it would appear from the Apostle's language that even the lamp of prophecy, shining in a dark place, was in two respects defective. "God spake in the prophets by divers portions and in divers manners." He spake in divers portions; that is, the revelation was broken, as the light was scattered before it was gathered into one source. Again, He spake in divers manners. Not only the revelation was fragmentary, but the separate portions were not of the same kind. The two defects were that the revelation lacked unity and was not homogeneous.

In contrast to the fragmentary character of the revelation, the Apostle speaks of the Son, in the second verse, as the centre of unity. He is the Heir and the Creator of all things. With the heterogeneous revelation in the prophets he contrasts, in the third verse, the revelation that takes its form from the peculiar nature of Christ's Sonship. He is the effulgence of God's glory, the very image of His substance; He upholds all things by the word of His power; and, having made purification of sins, He took His seat on the right hand of the Majesty on high.

Let us examine a little more closely the double comparison made by the Apostle between the revelation given to the fathers and that which we have received.

First, the previous revelation was in portions. The Old Testament has no centre, from which all its

wonderful and varied lights radiate, till we find its
unity in the New Testament and read Jesus Christ into
it.　God scattered the revelations over many centuries,
line upon line, precept after precept, here a little and
there a little.　He spread the knowledge of Himself
over the ages of a nation's history, and made the
development of one people the medium whereby to
communicate truth.　This of itself, if nothing more had
been told us, is a magnificent conception.　A nation's
early struggles, bitter failures, ultimate triumph, the
appearance within it of warriors, prophets, poets, saints,
used by the Spirit of God to reveal the invisible!
Sometimes revelation would make but one advance in
an age.　We might almost imagine that God's truth
from the lips of His prophets was found at times too
overpowering.　It was crushing frail humanity.　The
Revealer must withdraw into silence behind the thick
veil, to give human nature time to breathe and recover
self-possession.　The occasional message of prophecy
resembles the suddenness of Elijah's appearances and
departures, and forms a strange contrast to the cease-
less stream of preaching in the Christian Church.

Still more strikingly does it contrast with the New
Testament, the greater book, yea the greatest of all
books.　Only two classes of men deny its supremacy.
They are those who do not know what real greatness
is, and those who disparage it as a literature that they

may be the better able to seduce foolish and shallow youths to reject it as a revelation. But honest and profound thinkers, even when they do not admit that it is the word of God, acknowledge it to be the greatest among the books of men.

Yet the New Testament was all produced—if we are forbidden to say "given"—in one age, not fifteen centuries. Neither was this one of the great ages of history, when genius seems to be almost contagious. Even Greece had at this time no original thinkers. Its two centuries of intellectual supremacy had passed away. It was the age of literary imitations and counterfeits. Yet it is in this age that the book which has most profoundly influenced the thought of all subsequent times made its appearance. How shall we account for the fact? The explanation is not that its writers were great men. However insignificant the writers, the mysterious greatness of the book pervades it all, and their lips are touched as with a live coal from the altar. Nothing will account for the New Testament but the other fact that Jesus of Nazareth had appeared among men, and that He was so great, so universal, so human, so Divine, that He contained in His own person all the truth that will ever be discovered in the book. Deny the incarnation of the Son of God, and you make the New Testament an insoluble enigma. Admit that Jesus is the Word, and that the Word is God, and the book becomes nothing more, nothing less, than the natural and befitting outcome of what He said and did and suffered. The mystery of the book is lost in the greater mystery of His person.

Here the second verse comes in, to tell us of this great Person, and how He unites in Himself the whole of God's revelation. He is appointed Heir of all things, and through Him God made the ages. He is the Alpha and the Omega, the first and the last, He which is, and which was, and which is to come,—the spring from which all the streams of time have risen and the sea into which they flow. But these are the two sides of all real knowledge; and revelation is nothing else than knowledge given by God. All the infinite variety of questions with which men interrogate nature may be reduced to two: Whence? and whither? As to the latter question, the investigation has not been in vain. We do know that, whatever the end will be, the whole universe rises from lower to higher forms. If one life perishes, it reappears in a higher life. It is the ultimate purpose of all which still remains unknown. But the Apostles declare that this interrogation is answered in Jesus Christ. Only that they speak, not of "ultimate purpose," but of "the appointed Heir." He is more than the goal of a development. He is the Son of the living God, and therefore the Heir of all the works and purposes of His

Father. He holds His position by right of sonship, and has it confirmed to Him as the reward of filial service.

The word "Heir" is an allusion to the promise made to Abraham. The reference, therefore, is not to the eternal relation between the Son and God, not to any lordship which the Son acquires apart from His assumption of humanity and atoning death. The idea conveyed by the word "Heir" will come again to the surface, more than once, in the Epistle. But everywhere the reference is to the Son's final glory as Redeemer. At the same time, the act of appointing Him Heir may have taken place before the world was. We must, accordingly, understand the revelation here spoken of to mean more especially the manifestation of God in the work of redemption. Of this work also Christ is the ultimate purpose. He is the Heir, to Whom the promised inheritance originally and ultimately belongs. It is this that befits Him to become the full and complete Revealer of God. He is the answer to the question, Whither? in reference to the entire range of redemptive thought and action.

Again, He, too, is the Creator. Many seek to discover the origin of all things by analysis. They trace the more complex to the less complex, the compound to its elements, and the higher developments of life to lower types. But to the theologian the real difficulty

does not lie here. What matter *whence*, if we are still
the same ? We know what we are. We *are* men.
We are capable of thinking, of sinning, of hating or
loving God. The problem is to account for these facts
of our spirit. What is the evolution of holiness ?
Whence came prayer, repentance, and faith ? But even
these questions Christianity professes to answer. It
answers them by solving still harder problems than
these. Do we ask who created the human spirit ?
The Gospel tells us who can sanctify man's inmost
being. Do we seek to know who made conscience ?
The New Testament proclaims One Who can purify
conscience and forgive the sin. To create is but a
small matter to Him Who can save. Jesus Christ is
that Saviour. He, therefore, is that Creator. In being
these things, He is the complete and final revelation
of God.

Second, previous revelations were given in divers
manners. God used many different means to reveal
Himself, as if He found them one after another inadequate. And how can a visible, material creation
sufficiently reveal the spiritual ? How can institutions
and systems reveal the personal, living God ? How
can human language even express spiritual ideas ?
Sometimes the means adopted appear utterly incon-
gruous. Will the great Spirit, the holy and good God,
speak to a prophet in the dreams of night ? Shall we

say that the man of God sees real visions when he
dreams an unreal dream ?   Or will an apparition of the
day more befittingly reveal God?   Has every substance
been possessed by the spirit of falsehood, so that the
Being of beings can only reveal His presence in un-
substantial phantoms ?   Has the waking life of intellect
become so entirely false to its glorious mission of
discovering truth that the God of truth cannot reveal
Himself to man, except in dreams and spectres ?   Yet
there was a time when it might be well for us to recall
our dreams, and wise to believe in spiritualism.   For a
dream might bring a real message from God, and
ecstasy might be the birth-throes of a new revelation.
Some of the good words of Scripture were at first a
dream.   In the midst of the confused fancies of the
brain, when reason is for a time dethroned, a truth
descends from heaven upon the prophet's spirit.   This
has been, but will never again take place.   The oracles
are dumb, and we shall not regret them.   We consult
no interpreter of dreams.   We seek not the seances of
necromancers.   Let the peaceful spirits of the dead
rest in God !   They had their trials and sorrows on
earth.   Rest, hallowed souls !   We do not ask you
to break the deep silence of heaven.   For God has
spoken unto us in a Son, Who has been made higher
than the heavens, and is as great as God.   Even the
Son need not, must not, come to earth a second time

to reveal the Father in mighty deeds and a mightier self-sacrifice. The revelation given is enough. "We will not say in our hearts, Who shall ascend into heaven? (that is, to bring Christ down:) or, Who shall descend into the abyss? (that is, to bring Christ up from the dead.) The word is nigh us, in our mouth, and in our heart: that is, the word of faith, which we preach." *

The final form of God's revelation of Himself is, therefore, perfectly homogeneous. The third verse explains that it is a revelation, not only in a Son, but in His Sonship. We learn what kind of Sonship is His, and how its glorious attributes qualify Him to be the perfect Revealer of God. Nevermore will a message be sent to men except in Jesus Christ. God, Who spake unto the fathers in divers manners, speaks to us in Him, Whose Sonship constitutes Him the effulgence of God's glory, the image of His substance, the Upholder of the universe, and, lastly, the eternal Redeemer and King.

1. He is the effulgence of God's glory. Many expositors prefer another rendering: "the reflection of His glory." This would mean that God's self-manifestation, shining on an external substance, is reflected, as from a mirror, and that this reflection is the Son of

* Rom. x. 6—8.

God. But such an expression does not convey a consistent idea. For the Son must be the substance from which the light is reflected. What truth there is in this rendering is more correctly expressed in the next clause: "the image of His substance." It is, therefore, much better to accept the rendering adopted in the Revised Version: "the effulgence of His glory." God's glory is the self-manifestation of His attributes, or, in other words, the consciousness which God has of His own infinite perfections. This implies the triune personality of God. But it does not imply a revelation of God to His creatures. The Son participates in that consciousness of the Divine perfections. But He also reveals God to men, not merely in deeds and in words, but in His person. He *is* the revelation. To declare this seems to be the Apostle's purpose in using the word "effulgence." It expresses "the essentially ministrative character of the person of the Son." * If a revelation will be given at all, His Sonship points Him out as the Interpreter of God's nature and purposes, inasmuch as He is essentially, because He is Son, the emanation or radiance of His glory.

2. He is the image of His substance. A solar ray reveals the light, but not completely, unless indeed it guides the eye back along its pencilled line to the orb

---

* Newman, *Arians*, p. 182 (ed. 1833).

of day. If the Son of God were only an effulgence,
Christ could still say that He Himself is the way to
the Father, but He could not add, " He that hath
seen Me hath seen the Father."* That the revelation
may be complete, the Son must be, in one sense, distinct from God, as well as one with Him. Apparently
this is the notion conveyed in the metaphor of the
" image." Both truths are stated together in the words
of Christ : " As the Father hath life in Himself, so
hath He given to the Son to have life *in Himself.*"†
If the Son is more than an effulgence, if He is "the
very image " of God's essence, nothing in God will
remain unrevealed. Every feature of His moral nature
will be delineated in the Son. If the Son is the exact
likeness of God and has a distinct mode of subsisting
He is capable of all the modifications in His form of
subsisting which may be necessary, in order to make
a complete revelation of God intelligible to men. It
is possible for Him to become man Himself. He is
capable of obedience, even of learning obedience by
suffering, and of acquiring power to succour by being
tempted. He can taste death. We might add, if we
were studying one of St. Paul's Epistles (which we are
not at present doing), that this distinction from God,
involved in His very Sonship, made Him capable of

---

* John xiv. 6, 9.   † John v. 26.

emptying Himself of the Divine form of subsisting and taking upon Him instead of it the form of a servant.   This power of meeting man's actual condition confers upon the Son the prerogative of being the complete and final revelation of God.

3. He upholds all things by the word of His power. This must be closely connected with the previous statement.   If the Son is the effulgence of God's glory and the express image of His essence, He is not a creature, but is the Creator.   The Son is so from God that He is God.   He so emanates from Him that He is a perfect and complete representation of His being.   He is not in such a manner an effulgence as to be only a manifestation of God, nor in such a manner an image as to be a creature of God.   But, in fellowship of nature, the essence of God is communicated to the Son in the distinctness of His mode of subsisting.   The Apostle's words fully justify—perhaps they suggested—the expressions in the Nicene and still earlier creeds, "God *of* God, Light *of* Light, very God *of* very God."   If this is His relation to God, it determines His relation to the universe, and the relation of the universe to God.   Philo had described the Word as an effulgence, and spoken also of Him as distinct from God.   But in Philo these two statements are inconsistent.   For the former means that the Word is an attribute of God, and the latter means that He is a creature.

The writer of the Epistle to the Hebrews says that the Word is not an attribute, but a perfect representation of God's essence. He says also that He is not a creature, but the Sustainer of all things. These statements are consistent. The one, in fact, implies the other ; and both together express the same conception which we find in St. John's Gospel : " In the beginning was the Word, and the Word was with God, and the Word was God. All things were made by Him ; and without Him was not anything made that hath been made."* It is also the teaching of St. Paul : " In Him were all things created, in the heavens and upon the earth, things visible and things invisible, whether thrones, or dominions, or principalities, or powers : all things have been created through Him, and unto Him ; and in Him all things consist." †

But the Apostle has a further motive in referring to the Son as Upholder of all things. As Creator and Sustainer He reveals God. He upholds all things *by the word of His power.* " The invisible things of God are perceived through the things which are made, even His everlasting power and Divinity." ‡ There is a revelation of God prior even to that given in the prophets.

4. Having made purification of sins, He took His seat on the right hand of the Majesty on high. We

---

* John i. 1, 3.　　† Col. i. 16, 17.　　‡ Rom. i. 20.

come now, at last, to the special revelation of God
which forms the subject of the Epistle. The Apostle
here states his central truth on its two sides. The
one side is Christ's priestly offering ; the other is His
kingly exaltation. We shall see as we proceed that
the entire structure of the Epistle rests on this great
conception,—the Son of God, the eternal Priest-King.
By introducing it at this early stage, the author gives
his readers the clue to what will very soon prove a
labyrinth. We must hold the thread firmly, if we
wish not to be lost in the maze. The subject of the
treatise is here given us. It is "The Son as Priest-
King the Revealer of God." The revelation is not in
words only, nor in external acts only, but in love, in
redemption, in opening heaven to all believers. It is
well termed a revelation. For the Priest-King has rent
the thick veil and opened the way to men to enter into
the true holiest place, so that they know God by
prayer and communion.

THE SON AND THE ANGELS.

HEBREWS i. 4—ii. 18.

CHAPTER II.

THE SON AND THE ANGELS.

THE most dangerous and persistent error against which the theologians of the New Testament had to contend was the doctrine of emanations. The persistence of this error lay in its affinity with the Christian conception of mediation between God and men; its danger sprang from its complete inconsistency with the Christian idea of the person and work of the Mediator. For the Hebrew conception of God, as the " I AM," tended more and more in the lapse of ages to sever Him from all immediate contact with created beings. It would be the natural boast of the Jews that Jehovah dwelt in unapproachable light. They would point to the contrast between Him and the human gods of the Greeks. An ever-deepening consciousness of sin and spiritual gloom would strengthen the conviction that the Lord abode behind the veil, and their conception of God would of necessity react on their consciousness of sin. If, therefore, God is the absolute Being—so argued the Gnostics of the day—He cannot be the actual Creator of the world. We must suppose the existence of an emanation or a series of emanations from God, every additional link in the chain being less Divine, until we arrive at the material universe, where the element of Divinity is entirely lost. These emanations are the angels, the only possible mediators between God and men. Some theories came to a stand at this point; others took a further step, and worshipped the angels, as the mediators also between men and God. Thus the angels were regarded as messengers or apostles from God and reconcilers or priests for men. St. Paul has already rejected these notions in his Epistle to the Colossians. He teaches that the Son of God's love is the visible image of the invisible God, prior to all creation and by right of primogeniture Heir of all, Creator of the highest angels, Himself being before they came into existence. Such He is before His assumption of humanity. But it pleased God that in Him, also as God-Man, all the plenitude of the Divine attributes should dwell; so that the Mediator is not an emanation, neither human nor Divine, but is Himself God and Man.*

Recent expositors have sufficiently proved that there was a Judaic element in the Colossian heresy. We

---

* Col. i. 15, 19.

need not, therefore, hesitate to admit that the Epistle
to the Hebrews contains references to the same error.
Our author acknowledges the existence of angels. He
declares that the Law was given through angels, which
is a point not touched upon more than once in the
Old Testament, but seemingly taken for granted, rather
than expressly announced, in the New. Stephen
reproaches the Jews, who had received the Law as
the ordinances of angels, with having betrayed and
murdered the Righteous One, of Whom the Law and
the prophets spake.* St. Paul, like the author of the
Epistle to the Hebrews, argues that the Law differs
from the promise in having been ordained through
angels, as mediators between the Lord and His people
Israel, whereas the promise was given by God, not
as a compact between two parties, but as the free act
of Him Who is one.† The main purpose of the first
and second chapters of our Epistle is to maintain the
superiority of the Son to the angels, of Him in Whom
God has spoken unto us to the mediators through
whom He gave the Law.

The defect of the doctrine of emanations was twofold. They are supposed to consist of a long chain of
intermediate beings. But the chain does not connect
at either end. God is still absolutely unapproachable

---

* Acts vii. 53.　　　　　† Gal. iii. 19.

by man; man is still inaccessible to God. It is in
vain new links are forged. The chain does not, and
never will, bring man and God together. The only
solution of the problem must be found in One Who is
God and Man; and this is precisely the doctrine of
our author, on the one hand, that the Revealer of God
is Son of God; and, on the other hand, that the Son
of God is our brother-man. The former statement is
proved, and a practical warning based upon it, in the
section that extends from chap. i. 4 to chap. ii. 4.
The latter is the subject of the section from chap.
ii. 5 to chap. ii. 18.

I. The Revealer of God Son of God.

"Having become by so much better than the angels, as He hath
inherited a more excellent name than they. For unto which of the
angels said He at any time,

> Thou art my Son,
> This day have I begotten Thee?

and again,

> I will be to Him a Father,
> And He shall be to Me a Son?

And when He again bringeth in the Firstborn into the world He saith,
And let all the angels of God worship Him. And of the angels He
saith,

> Who maketh His angels winds,
> And His ministers a flame of fire:

but of the Son *He saith*,

> Thy throne, O God, is for ever and ever;
> And the sceptre of uprightness is the sceptre of Thy kingdom.

Thou hast loved righteousness, and hated iniquity ;
Therefore God, Thy God, hath anointed Thee
With the oil of gladness above Thy fellows.

And,

Thou, Lord, in the beginning hast laid the foundation of the earth,
And the heavens are the works of Thy hands :
They shall perish ; but Thou continuest :
And they all shall wax old as doth a garment ;
And as a mantle shalt Thou roll them up,
As a garment, and they shall be changed :
But Thou art the same,
And Thy years shall not fail.

But of which of the angels hath He said at any time,

Sit Thou on My right hand,
Till I make Thine enemies the footstool of Thy feet ?

Are they not all ministering spirits, sent forth to do service for the sake of them that shall inherit salvation ?

Therefore we ought to give the more earnest heed to the things that were heard, lest haply we drift away *from them.* For if the word spoken through angels proved steadfast, and every transgression and disobedience received a just recompense of reward ; how shall we escape, if we neglect so great salvation? which having at the first been spoken through the Lord, was confirmed unto us by them that heard ; God also bearing witness with them, both by signs and wonders, and by manifold powers, and by gifts of the Holy Ghost, according to His own will " (Heb. i. 4—ii. 4, R.V.).

Christ is Son of God, not in the sense in which angels, as a class of beings, are designated by this name, but as He Who has taken His seat on the right hand of the Majesty on high. The greatness of His position is proportionate to the excellency of the name

of Son.   This name He has not obtained by favour nor
attained by effort, but inherited by indefeasible right.
Josephus says that the Essenes forbade their disciples
to divulge the names of the angels.   But He Who has
revealed God has been revealed Himself.   He is Son.
Which of the angels was ever so addressed ?   To speak
of the angels as sons and yet say that not one of them
individually is a son may be self-contradictory in
words, but the thought is consistent and true.

From the pre-existent Son, regarded as the idealised
theocratic King, the Apostle passes to the incarnate
Christ, returning to the world which He has redeemed,
and out of which He brings * many sons of God unto
glory.   God brings Him also in as the First-begotten
among these many brethren.   But our Lord Himself
describes His coming.   " The Son of man shall come
in His glory, and all the angels with Him." †   In
allusion to this saying of Christ, the Apostle applies to
His second advent the words which in the Septuagint
Version of the Old Testament are a summons to all
the angels to worship Jehovah.   They are the Son's
ministers.   Like swift winds, they convey His
messages ; or they carry destruction at His bidding,
like a flame of fire.   But the Son is enthroned God
for ever.   The sceptre of righteousness, by whomso-

---

* ἀγαγόντα.   † Matt. xxv. 31.

ever borne, is the sceptre of His kingdom ; all thrones and powers, human and angelic, hold sway under Him. They are His fellows, and participate only in His royal gladness, Whose joy surpasses theirs.

The author reverts to the Son's pre-incarnate exist-ence. The Son created earth and heaven, and, for that reason, He remains when the works of His hand wax old, as a garment. Creation is the vesture of the Son. In all the changes of nature the Son puts off a garment, while He remains unchanged Himself.

Finally, our author glances at the triumphant con-summation, when God will do for His Son what He will not do for the angels. For He will make His enemies the footstool of His feet, as the reward of His redemptive work. The angels have no enemy to conquer. Neither are they the authors of our redemp-tion. Yea, they are not even the redeemed. The Son is the Heir of the throne. Men are the heirs of salvation. Must we, then, quite exclude the angels from all present activity in the kingdom of the Son ? Do they altogether belong to a past epoch in the development of God's revelation ? Must we say of them, as astronomers speak of the moon, that they are dead worlds ? Shall we not rather find a place for them in the spirit-world corresponding to the office filled in the sphere of nature by the works of God's hands ? God has His earthly ministers. Are not the angels ministering spirits? The Apostle puts the question tentatively. But the pious instinct of the Church and of good men has answered, Yes. For salvation has created a new form of service for which nature is not fitted. The narrative of the Son's own life on earth suggests the same reply. For an angel appeared unto Him in Gethsemane and strengthened Him.* It is true that the Son Himself is the Minister of the sanctuary. He alone serves in the holiest place. But may not the angels be *sent forth* to minister? Salvation is the work of the Son. But shall we not say that the angels perform a service for the Son, which is possible only because of men who are now on the eve of inheriting that salvation?

We must beware of minimising the significance of the Apostle's words. If he means by "Son" merely an official designation, where is the difference between the Son and the angels? The only definition of "Son" that will satisfy the argument is "God the Revealer of God." Sabellius said, "The Word is not the Son." The contrary doctrine is necessary to give any value to the reasoning of our Epistle. The Revealer is Son; and the Son, in order to be the full Revealer, must be "of the essence of the Father," inasmuch as God only can perfectly reveal God. This

---

* Luke xxii. 43. The genuineness of the verse is somewhat doubtful.

is so vital to the Apostle's argument that he need not
hesitate to use a term in reference to the Son which
in another connection might be liable to be misunderstood, as if it expressed the theory of emanation.
The Son is "the effulgence" of the Father's glory,
or, in the words of the Nicene Creed, He is "Light
out of Light." It is safe to use such words when our
very argument demands that He should also be "the
distinct impress of His substance,"—"very God out
of very God."

The Apostle has now laid the foundation of his
great argument. He has shown us the Son as the
Revealer of God. This done, he at once introduces
his first practical warning. It is his manner. He
does not, like St. Paul, first conclude the argumentative
portion of his Epistle, and afterwards heap precept on
precept in words of warning, sympathy, or encouragement. Our author alternates argument with exhortation. The Epistle wears to a superficial reader the
appearance of a mosaic. The truth is that no book in
the New Testament is more thoroughly or more skil-
fully welded into one piece from beginning to end.
But the danger was imminent, and urgent warning
was needed at every step. One truth was better fitted
to drive home one lesson, and another argument to
enforce another.

The first danger of the Hebrew Christians would

arise from indifference. The first warning of the Apostle is, Take care that you do not drift.* In the Son as the Revealer of God we have a sure anchorage. Let us fasten the vessel to its moorings. That the Son has revealed God is beyond question. The fact is well assured. For the message of salvation has been proclaimed by the Lord Jesus Himself. It has run its course down to the writer of the Epistle and his readers through the testimony of eye-witnesses and ear-witnesses. God Himself has borne witness with these faithful men by signs and wonders and divers manifestations of power, yea by giving the Holy Ghost to each one severally according to His own will. The last words are not to be neglected. The apparent arbitrariness of His sovereign will in the distribution of the Spirit lends force to the proof, by pointing to the direct, personal action of God in this great concern.

But the warning is based, not simply on the fact of a revelation, but on the greatness of the Revealer. The Law was given through angels, and the Law was not transgressed with impunity. How, then, shall we escape God's anger if we contemptuously neglect a salvation so great that no one less than the Son could have wrought or revealed it?

* μὴ παραρυῶμεν (ii. 1).

Observe the emphatic notions. Salvation is contrasted
with law.   It is a greater sin to despise God's free,
merciful offer of eternal life than to transgress the
commandments of His justice.   There may be emphasis
also on the certainty of the proof.   The word spoken
by angels was firmly assured, and, because no man could
shelter under the plea that the heavenly authority of the
message was doubtful, disobedience met with unspar-
ing retribution.   But the Gospel is proved to be of
God by still more abundant evidence,—the personal
testimony of the Lord Jesus, the witness of those who
heard Him, and the cumulative argument of gifts and
miracles.   While these truths are emphatic, more
important than all is the fact that the Son is the Giver
of this salvation.   The thought seems to be that God
is jealous for the honour of His Son.   Our Lord Himself teaches this, and the form which it assumes in
His parable implies that He speaks, not as a specula-
tive moralist, but as One Who knows God's heart:
"Last of all he sent unto them his son, saying,
They will reverence my son."   But when Christ asks
His hearers what the lord of the vineyard will do
unto those wicked husbandmen, the manner of their
reply shows that they only half understand His meaning or else pretend not to see the point of His question.
They acknowledge the husbandmen's wickedness, but
profess that it consists largely in not rendering to the

owner the fruits in their season, as if, forsooth, their wickedness in killing their master's son had not thrust their dishonesty quite out of sight.* The Apostle, too, appeals to his readers,† evidently in the belief that they would at once feel the force of his argument, whether trampling under foot the Son of God did not deserve sorer punishment than despising the law of Moses. Christ and the Apostle speak in the spirit of the second Psalm : " Thou art My Son. Ask of Me, and I shall give Thee the heathen for Thine inheritance, and the uttermost parts of the earth for Thy posses- sion. . . . Kiss the Son !" Now, if Christ adopts this language, it is not mere metaphor, but is a truth con- cerning God's moral nature. Resentment must, in some sense or other, belong to God's Fatherhood. The doctrine of the Trinity implies the necessary and eternal altruism of the Divine nature. It would not be true to say that the God of the Christians was less jealous than the God of the Hebrews. He is still the living God. It is a fearful thing to fall into His hands. He will still vindicate the majesty of His law. But now He has spoken unto us in One Who is Son. The Judge of all is not a mere official Administrator, but a Father. The place occupied in the Old Testament by the Law is now filled by the Son.

---

* Matt. xxi. 33, sqq.   † Heb. x. 29.

II. The Son the Representative of Man.

" For not unto angels did He subject the world to come, whereof we speak. But one hath somewhere testified, saying,

> What is man, that Thou art mindful of him?
> Or the son of man, that Thou visitest him?
> Thou madest him a little lower than the angels ;
> Thou crownedst him with glory and honour,
> And didst set him over the works of Thy hands :
> Thou didst put all things in subjection under his feet.

For in that He subjected all things unto him, He left nothing that is not subject to him. But now we see not yet all things subjected to him. But we behold Him Who hath been made a little lower than the angels, *even* Jesus, because of the suffering of death crowned with glory and honour, that by the grace of God He should taste death for every *man*. For it became Him, for Whom are all things, and through Whom are all things, in bringing many sons unto glory, to make the Author of their salvation perfect through sufferings. For both He that sanctifieth and they that are sanctified are all of one : for which cause He is not ashamed to call them brethren, saying,

> I will declare Thy name unto My brethren,
> In the midst of the congregation will I sing Thy praise

And again, I will put My trust in Him.   And again, Behold, I and the children which God hath given Me.   Since then the children are sharers in flesh and blood, He also Himself in like manner partook of the same ; that through death He might bring to nought him that had the power of death, that is, the devil ; and might deliver all them who through fear of death were all their lifetime subject to bondage.   For verily not of angels doth He take hold, but He taketh hold of the seed of Abraham.   Wherefore it behoved Him in all things to be made like unto His brethren, that He might be a merciful and faithful High-priest in things pertaining to God, to make propitiation for the sins of the people.   For in that He Himself hath suffered being tempted, He is able to succour them that are tempted " (HEB. ii. 5—18, R.V.).

The Son is better than the angels, not only because He is the Revealer of God, but also because He represents man. We have to do with more than spoken promises. The salvation through Christ raises man to a new dignity, and bestows upon him a new authority. God calls into existence a "world to come," and puts that world in subjection, not to angels, but to man.

The passage on the consideration of which we now enter is difficult, because the interpretation offered by some of the best expositors, though at first sight it has the appearance of simplicity, really introduces confusion into the argument. They think the words of the Psalmist,* as applied by the Apostle, refer to Christ only. But the Psalmist evidently contrasts the frailty of man with the authority bestowed upon him by Jehovah. Mortal man has been set over the works of God's hand. Man is for a little inferior to the angels; yet he is crowned with glory and honour. The very contrast between his frailty and his dignity exalts the name of his Creator, Who judges not as we judge. For He confronts His blasphemers with the lisping of children, and weak man He crowns king of creation, in order to put to shame the wisdom of the world.†

We cannot suppose that this is said of Christ, the Son of God. But there are two expressions in the

---

* Ps. viii. 4.   † Ps. viii. ?.

Psalm that suggested to St. Paul* and the author of this
Epistle a Messianic reference.   The one is the name
"Son of man;" the other is the action ascribed to
God: "Thou hast made him lower than the angels."
The word † used by the Seventy, whose translation the
Apostle here and elsewhere adopts, means, not, as the
Hebrew, "to create lower," but "to bring from a more
exalted to a humbler condition."   Christ appropriated
to Himself the title of "Son of man;" and "to lower
from a higher to a less exalted position" applies only
to the Son of God, Whose pre-existence is taught by
the Apostle in chap i.   The point of the Apostle's
application of the Psalm must, therefore, be that in
Christ alone have the Psalmist's words been fulfilled.
The Psalmist was a prophet, and testified.‡   In addition
to the witnesses previously mentioned,§ the Apostle
cites the evidence from prophecy.   An inspired seer,
"seeing this beforehand, spake of Christ," not primarily,
but in a mystery now explained in the New Testament.
The distinction also between crowning with glory and
putting all things under his feet holds true only of
Christ.   The Psalmist, we admit, appears to identify
them.   But the relevancy of the Apostle's use of the
Psalm lies in the distinction between these two things.

---

* 1 Cor. xv 27.　　　　‡ Cf. Acts ii. 30.
† ηλιττωσας.　　　　§ Chap. ii. 4.

The creature man may be said to be crowned with
glory and honour by receiving universal dominion and
by the subjection of all things under his feet. " But
we see not yet all things put under him ;" and,
consequently, we see not man crowned with glory and
honour. The words of the Psalmist have apparently
failed of fulfilment or were at best only poetical
exaggeration. But Him Who was actually translated
from a higher to a lower place than that of angels, from
heaven to earth—that is to say, Jesus, the meek and
lowly Man of Nazareth—we see crowned with glory
and honour. He has ascended to heaven and sat down
on the right hand of the Majesty on high. So far the
prophecy has come true, but only so far. All things
have not yet been put under Him. He is still waiting
till He has put all enemies, even the last enemy, which
is death, under His feet. As, then, the glory and
honour are bestowed on man through his Representative,
Jesus, so also dominion is given him only through
Jesus ; and the glory comes only with the dominion.
Every honour that falls to man's share is won for him
by the victory of Christ over an enemy. This is the
nearest approach in our Epistle to the Pauline conception
of Christ as the second Adam.

But is there any connection between Christ's victory
and His being made lower than the angels ? When the
Psalmist describes the great dignity conferred on frail

man, he sees only the contrast between the dignity and the frailty.   He can only wonder and worship in observing the incomprehensible paradox of God's dealings with man.   The Apostle, on the other hand, fathoms this mystery.   He gives the reasons for the strange connection of power and feebleness, not indeed in reference to man as a creature, but in reference to the Man Christ Jesus.   Apart from Christ the problem that struck the Psalmist with awe remains unsolved. But in Christ's incarnation we see why man's glory and dominion rest on humiliation.

1. Christ's humiliation involved a propitiatory death for every man, and He is crowned with glory and honour that His propitiation may prove effectual: "that He may have tasted * death for every man."   By His glory we must mean the self-manifestation of His person.   Honour is the authority bestowed upon Him by God.   Both are the result of His suffering death, or rather the suffering of His death.   He is glorified, not simply because He suffered, but because His suffering was of a certain kind and quality.   It was a propitiatory suffering.   Christ Himself prayed His Father to glorify Him with His own self with the glory He had with the Father before the world was.†   This glory was His by right of Sonship.   But He receives

---

* γεύσηται (ii. 9).   † John xvii. 5.

from His Father another glory, not by right, but by God's grace.* It consists in having His death accepted and acknowledged as an adequate propitiation for the sins of men. In this verse the great conception of atonement, which hereafter will fill so large a place in the Epistle, is introduced, not at present for its own sake, but in order to show the superiority of Christ to the angels. He is greater than they because He is the representative Man, to Whom, and not to the angels, the world to come has been put in subjection. But the Psalmist has taught us that man's greatness is connected with humiliation. This connection is realised in Christ, Whose exaltation is the Divine acceptance of the propitiation wrought in the days of His humiliation, and the means of giving it effect.

2. Christ's glory consists in being Leader † of His people, and for such leadership He was fitted by the discipline of humiliation. There is no incongruity in the works of God because He is Himself the ground of their being ‡ and the instrument of His own action.§ *Every* adaptation of means to an end would not become God, though it might befit man. But this became Him for Whom and through Whom are all things. When He crowns man with glory and honour, He does this, not by an external ordinance merely, but by an inward

---

* χάριτι   † ἀρχηγόν (ii. 10).   ‡ δι᾿ ὅν.   § δι᾿ οὗ.

fitness. He deals, not with an abstraction, but with individual men, whom He makes His sons and prepares for their glory and honour by the discipline of sons. "For what son is there whom his father does not discipline?" * Thus it is more true to say that God leads His sons to glory than to say that He bestows glory upon them. It follows that the representative Man, through Whom these many sons are glorified, must Himself pass through like discipline, that, on behalf of God, He may become their Leader and the Captain of their salvation. It became God to endow the Son, in Whose Sonship men are adopted as sons of God, with inward fitness, through sufferings, to lead them on to their destined glory. Perhaps the verse contains an allusion to Moses or Joshua, the leaders of the Lord's redeemed to the rich land and large. If so, the author is preparing his readers for what he has yet to say.

3. Christ's glory consists in power to consecrate † men to God, and this power springs from His consciousness of brotherhood with them. But, first of all, the author thinks it necessary to prove that Christ has a deep consciousness of brotherhood with men. He cites Christ's own words from prophetic Scripture.‡ For Christ has vowed unto the Lord, Who has delivered Him, that He will declare God's name unto His

---

* Chap. xii. 7.   † ὁ ἁγιάζων (ii. 11).   ‡ Ps. xxii. 22.

brethren.   Here the pith of the argument is quite **as**
much in the vow to reveal God to them as in His **giving**
them the name of brethren.   He is so drawn in love **to**
them that He is impelled to speak to them about **the**
Father.   Yea, in the midst of the Church, as if **He**
were one of the congregation, He will praise **God.**
They praise God for His Son ; the Son joins in **the**
praise, as being thankful for the privilege of being their
Saviour, while they offer their thanks for the joy of
being saved.   That is not all.   Christ puts His trust
in God.   So human is He that, conscious of utter
weakness, He leans on God, as the feeblest of His
brethren.   Finally, His triumphant joy at the safety
of His redeemed ones arises from this consciousness
of brotherhood.   "Behold, I and the children" (of
God) "which God hath given Me." *   The Apostle
does not fear to apply to Christ what Isaiah † spoke in
reference to himself and his disciples, the children of
the prophet.   Christ's brotherhood with men assumes
the form of identifying Himself with His prophetic
servants.   Evidently He is not ashamed of His
brethren, though, like Joseph, He has reason to be
ashamed of them for their sin.   The expression means
that He glories in them, because His assumption of
humanity has consecrated them.   For this consecration

---

* Chap. ii. 13.   † Isa. viii. 18.

springs from union. We do not, for our part, understand this as a general proposition, of which the
sanctifying power of Christ is an illustration. No other
instance of such a thing exists. Yet the Apostle does
not prove the statement. He appeals to the intelligence
and conscience of his readers to acknowledge its truth.
Whether we understand the word "sanctification" in
the sense of moral consecration through an atonement
or in the sense of holy character, it springs from union.
Christ cannot sanctify by a creative word or by an act
of power. Neither can His power to sanctify be trans-
mitted by God to the Son externally, in the same way
in which the Creator bestows on nature its vital, fer-
tilising energy. Christ must derive His power to
sanctify through His Sonship, and men must become
sons of God that they may be sanctified through the
Son. Our passage adds Christ's brotherhood. He
that consecrates, therefore, and they that are consecrated are united together, first, by being born of the
same Divine Father, and, second, by having the same
human nature. Here, again, the chain connects at
both ends : on the side of God and on the side of man.
Now to have dwelling in Him the power of consecrating
men to God is so great an endowment that Christ may
dare even to glory in the brotherhood that brings with
it such a gift.

4. Christ's glory manifests itself in the destruction of

Satan, who had the power of death, and his destruction
is accomplished through death.* The children of God
have every one his share of blood and flesh, which
means vital, mortal humanity. Blood signifies life, and
flesh the mortality of that life. They are, therefore,
subject to disease and death. But to the Hebrews
disease and death involved vastly more than physical
suffering and the termination of man's earthly existence.
They had their angel, by which is meant that they
had a moral significance. They were spiritual forces,
wielded by a messenger of God. This angel was
Satan. But, following the lead of the later Jewish
theology, our author explains who Satan really is. He
identifies him with the evil spirit, who from envy, says
the Book of Wisdom, brought death into the world.
To make clear this identification, he adds the words,
"that is, the devil." The reference to Satan is sufficient to show that the writer of the Epistle means by
"the power of death" power to inflict it and keep men
in its terrible grasp. But the difficulty is to understand how the devil is destroyed through death.
Evidently the death of Christ is meant; we may
paraphrase the Apostle's expression by rendering,
"through *His* death." At first glance, the words,
taken in connection with the reference to Christ's

* Chap. ii. 14.

humanity, seem to favour the doctrine, propounded by many writers in the early ages of the Church, that God delivered His Son to Satan as the price of man's release from his rightful possession. Such a notion is utterly inconsistent with the dominant idea of the Epistle : the priestly character of Christ's death. A Hebrew Christian could not conceive the high-priest entering the holiest place to offer a redemptive sacrifice to the spirit of evil. Indeed, the advocates of this strange theory of the Atonement admitted as much when they described Christ as outwitting the devil or escaping from his hands by persuasion. But the doctrine is quite as inconsistent with the passage before us, which represents the death of Christ as the *destruction* of the Evil One. Power faces power. Christ is the Captain of salvation. His leadership of men implies conflict with their enemy and ultimate victory. Death was a spiritual conception. Here lay its power. Deliverance from the crushing bondage of its fear could come only through the great High-priest. Priesthood was the basis of Christ's power. We shall soon see that Christ is the Priest-King. The Apostle even now anticipates what he has hereafter to say on the relation of the priesthood to the kingly power. For as Priest Christ delivers men from guilt of conscience and, by so doing, delivers them from their fear of death ; as King He destroys him who had the power to destroy. He is "death of death and hell's destruction." It has been well said that the two terrors from which none but Christ can deliver men are guilt of sin and fear of death. The latter is the offspring of the former. When the conscience of sin is no more, dread of death yields to peace and joy.

In these four ways is the glory of Christ connected with humiliation, and thus will the prophecy of the Psalmist find its fulfilment in the representative Man, Jesus. His humiliation implied propitiation, moral discipline, conscious brotherhood, and subjection to him who had the power of death. His glory consisted in the effectiveness of the propitiation, in leadership of His people, in consecration of His brethren, in the destruction of the devil.

But an interesting view of the passage has been proposed by Hofmann, and accepted by at least one thoughtful theologian of our country. They consider that the Apostle identifies the humiliation and the glory. In the words of Dr. Bruce,* "Christ's whole state of exinanition was not only worthy to be rewarded by a subsequent state of exaltation, but was in itself invested with moral sublimity and dignity." The idea has considerable fascination. We cannot set it aside by saying that it is modern, seeing that the Apostle himself

---

* *Humiliation of Christ,* p. 46.

speaks of the office of high-priest as an honour and a glory.* Yet we are compelled to reject it as an explanation of the passage. The Apostle is showing that the Psalmist's statement respecting man is realised only in the Man Christ Jesus. The difficulty was to connect man's low estate and man's glory and dominion. But if the Apostle means that voluntary humiliation for the sake of others is the glory, some men besides Jesus Christ might have been mentioned in whom the words of the Psalm find their accomplishment. The difference between Jesus and other good men would only be a difference of degree. Such a conclusion would very seriously weaken the force of the Apostle's reasoning.

In bringing his most skilful and original argument to a close, the Apostle recapitulates. He has said that the world to come,—the world of conscience and of spirit,—has been put in subjection to man, not to angels, and that this implies the incarnation of the Son of God. This thought the Apostle repeats in another, but very striking, form : " For verily He taketh not hold of angels, but He taketh hold of the seed of Abraham." Though the old versions were incorrect in so rendering the words as to make them express the fact of the Incarnation, the verse is a reference to the

---

* Chap. v. 4, 5.

Incarnation, described, however, as Christ's strong grasp * of man. By becoming man He takes hold of humanity, as with a mighty hand, and that part by which He grasps humanity is the seed of Abraham, to whom the promise was made.

Four points of connection between the glory of Christ and His humiliation have been mentioned. In his recapitulation, the Apostle sums all up in two. The one is that Christ is Priest; the other is that He succours them that are tempted. His propitiatory death and His bringing to nought the power of Satan are included in the notion of priesthood. The moral discipline that made Him our Leader and the sense of brotherhood that made Him Sanctifier render Him able to succour the tempted. Even this also, as will be fully shown by the Apostle in a subsequent chapter, is contained in His priesthood. For He only can make propitiation, Whose heart is full of tender pity and steeled only against pity for Himself by reason of His dauntless fidelity to others.

Thus is the Son better than the angels.

---

* ἐπιλαμβάνεται (ii. 16).

FUNDAMENTAL ONENESS OF THE DISPENSATIONS.

HEBREWS iii. 1—iv. 13 (R.V.).

" Wherefore, holy brethren, partakers of a heavenly calling, consider the Apostle and High-priest of our confession, *even* Jesus ; who was faithful to Him that appointed Him, as also was Moses in all his house. For He hath been counted worthy of more glory than Moses, by so much as he that built the house hath more honour than the house. For every house is builded by some one ; but He that built all things is God. And Moses indeed was faithful in all his house as a servant, for a testimony of those things which were afterward to be spoken ; but Christ as a Son, over His house ; Whose house are we, if we hold fast our boldness and the glorying of our hope firm unto the end. Wherefore, even as the Holy Ghost saith,

> To-day if ye shall hear His voice,
> Harden not your hearts, as in the provocation,
> Like as in the day of the temptation in the wilderness,
> Wherewith your fathers tempted *Me* by proving *Me*,
> And saw My works forty years.
> Wherefore I was displeased with this generation,
> And said, They do alway err in their heart :
> But they did not know My ways ;
> As I sware in My wrath,
> They shall not enter into My rest.

Take heed, brethren, lest haply there shall be in any one of you an evil heart of unbelief, in falling away from the living God : but exhort one another day by day, so long as it is called to-day ; lest any one of you be hardened by the deceitfulness of sin : for we are become partakers of Christ, if we hold fast the beginning of our confidence firm unto the end : while it is said,

> To-day if ye shall hear His voice,
> Harden not your hearts, as in the provocation.

For who, when they heard, did provoke? nay, did not all they that

4

came out of Egypt by Moses? And with whom was He displeased forty years? was it not with them that sinned, whose carcases fell in the wilderness? And to whom sware He that they should not enter into His rest, but to them that were disobedient? And we see that they were not able to enter in because of unbelief.

Let us fear therefore, lest haply, a promise being left of entering into His rest, any one of you should seem to have come short of it. For indeed we have had good tidings preached unto us, even as also they: but the word of hearing did not profit them, because they were not united by faith with them that heard. For we which have believed do enter into that rest; even as He hath said,

> As I sware in My wrath,
> They shall not enter into My rest:

although the works were finished from the foundation of the world. For He hath said somewhere of the seventh *day* on this wise, And God rested on the seventh day from all His works; and in this *place* again,

> They shall not enter into My rest.

Seeing therefore it remaineth that some should enter thereinto, and they to whom the good tidings were before preached failed to enter in because of disobedience, He again defineth a certain day, saying in David, after so long a time, To-day, as it hath been before said,

> To-day if ye shall hear His voice,
> Harden not your hearts.

For if Joshua had given them rest, he would not have spoken afterward of another day. There remaineth therefore a sabbath rest for the people of God. For he that is entered into his rest hath himself also rested from his works, as God did from His. Let us therefore give diligence to enter into that rest, that no man fall after the same example of disobedience. For the word of God is living, and active, and sharper than any two-edged sword, and piercing even to the dividing of soul and spirit, of both joints and marrow, and quick to discern the thoughts and intents of the heart. And there is no creature that is not manifest in His sight: but all things are naked and laid open before the eyes of Him with Whom we have to do."

CHAPTER III.

FUNDAMENTAL ONENESS OF THE DISPENSATIONS.

THE broad foundation of Christianity has now been laid in the person of the Son, God-Man. In the subsequent chapters of the Epistle this doctrine is made to throw light on the mutual relations of the two dispensations.

The first deduction is that the Mosaic dispensation was itself created by Christ; that the threats and promises of the Old Testament live on into the New; that the central idea of the Hebrew religion, the idea of the Sabbath rest, is realised in its inmost meaning in Christ only; that the word of God is ever full of living energy. Hereafter the Apostle will not be slow to expose the wide difference between the two dispensations. But it is equally true and not less important that the old covenant was the vesture of truths which remain when the garment has been changed.

At the outset the writer's tone is influenced by this doctrine. He turns his treatise unconsciously into an epistle. He addresses his readers as brethren, holy

indeed, but not holy after the pattern of their former
exclusiveness ; for their holiness is inseparably linked
with their common brotherhood.   They are partakers
with the Gentile Churches in a heavenly call.   Startling
words !   Hebrews holy in virtue of their sharing
with Greeks and barbarians, bond and free, in a
common call from high Heaven, which sees all earth
as a level plain beneath !   The middle wall of partition
has been broken down to the ground.   Yet soothing
words, and full of encouragement !   The Apostle and
his readers were standing near the end of the Apostolic
age, when the Hebrew Christians were despondent,
weak, and despised, both by reason of national
calamities and because of their inferiority to their
sister Churches among the Gentiles.   The Apostle does
not bluntly assure them of their equality, but gently
addresses them as partakers of a heavenly call.   His
words are the reverse of St. Paul's language to the
Ephesians, who are reminded that the Gentiles are
partakers in the privileges of Israel.   Those who sometimes were far off have been made nigh ; the strangers
and sojourners are henceforth fellow-citizens with the
saints and of the household of God.   Here, on the
contrary, Hebrew Christians are encouraged with the
assurance that they partake in the privileges of all
believers.   If the wild olive tree has been grafted in
among the branches and made partaker of the root,

the branches, broken off that the wild olive might be grafted in, are themselves in consequence grafted into their own olive tree. Through God's mercy to the Gentiles, Israel also has obtained mercy.

The Apostle addresses them with affection. But his behest is sharp and urgent : " Consider the Apostle and High-priest of our profession, Jesus." Consider intently, or, to borrow a modern word that has some-times been abused, Realise Jesus. Dwell not with abstractions and theories. Fear not imaginary dangers. Make Jesus Christ a reality before the eyes of your mind. To do this well will be more convincing than external evidences. To behold the glory of the temple, linger not to admire the strong buttresses without, but enter. Realisation of Christ may be said to be the gist of the whole Epistle.

This spiritual vision is not ecstasy. We realise Christ as Apostle and as High-priest. We behold Him when His words are a message to us from God, and when He carries our supplications to God. Revela-tion and prayer are the two opposite poles of com-munion with the Father. The dispensation of Moses rested on these two pillars,—apostleship and priest-hood. But the fundamental conceptions of the Old Testament centre in Jesus. Though our author has distinguished between God's revelation in the prophets and His revelation in a Son, he teaches also that even the prophets received their message through the Son. Though he contrasts in what follows of the Epistle the high-priesthood of Aaron with Christ's, still he regards Aaron's office as utterly meaningless apart from Christ. The words "Apostle and High-priest" pave the way, therefore, to the most prominent truth in this section of the Epistle : that whatever is best in the Old Testament has been assimilated and inspired with new energy by the Gospel.

1. To begin, we must understand the actual position of the founders of the two dispensations. Neither Moses nor Christ set about originating, designing, constructing, from his own impulse and for his own purposes. Both acted for God, and were consciously under His directing eye.* "It is required in stewards that a man be found faithful."† They have but to obey, and leave the unity and harmony of the plan to another. To use an illustration, every house is built by some one or other.‡ The design has been conceived in the brain of the architect. He is the real builder, though he employs masons and joiners to put the materials together according to his plan. This applies to the subject in hand ; for God is the Architect of all things. He realises His own ideas as well through the seeming originality of thinkers as

---

* Chap. iii. 2.   † 1 Cor. iv. 2.   ‡ Chap. iii. 4.

through the willing obedience of workers. Now, the dispensation of the old covenant was one part of God's design. To build this portion of the house He found a faithful servant in Moses. The dispensation of the new covenant is but another, though more excellent, part of the same design; and Jesus was not less faithful to finish the structure. The unity of the design was in the mind of God.

Moses was faithful when he refused the treasures of Egypt, and chose affliction with the people of God and the reproach of His Christ. He was faithful when he chid the people in the wilderness for their unbelief, and when he interceded for them again with God. Christ also was faithful to His God when He despised the shame and endured the Cross.

Yet we must acknowledge a difference. God has accounted Jesus worthy of greater honour than Moses, inasmuch as Moses was part of the house, and that part the pre-existent Christ erected. Moses was "made" all that he became by Christ, but Christ was "made"* all that He became—God-Man—by God. Moreover, though Moses was greater than all the other servants of God before Christ, because they were placed in subordinate positions, while he was faithful in the *whole* house, yet even he was but a servant,

---

* ποιήσαντι

whereas Christ was Son. Moses was in the house, it is true; but the Son was placed over the house. The work which Moses had to do was to uphold the authority of the Son, to witness, that is, to the things which would afterwards be spoken unto us by God in His Son, Jesus Christ.*

The Apostle seems to delight in his illustration of the house, and continues to use it with a fresh meaning. This house, or, if you please, this household, are we Christians. We are the house in which Moses showed the utmost faithfulness as servant. We are the circumcision, we the true Israel of God. If, then, we turn away from Christ to Moses, that faithful servant himself will have none of us. That we may be God's house, we must lay fast hold of our Christian confidence and the boasting of our hope out-and-out to the end.

2. Again, the threatenings of the Old Testament for disobedience to God apply with full force to apostasy from Christ. They are the authoritative voice of the Holy Spirit. The Apostle is reminded by the words which he has just used, " We are God's house," of the Psalmist's joyful exclamation, " He is our God, and we are the people of His pasture, and the sheep of His hand." † Then follows in the Psalm a warning, which the Apostle considers it equally necessary to address to

---

* Chap. iii. 5.   † Ps. xcv. 7, sqq.

the Hebrew Christians : "To-day, if indeed you still hear His voice (for it is possible He may no longer speak), harden not your hearts, as you did in Meribah, rightly called,—the place of contention. Your fathers, far from trusting Me when I put them to the test, turned upon Me and put Me to the test, and that although they saw My works during forty years." Forty years,—ominous number ! The readers would at once call to mind that forty years within a little had now passed since their Lord had gone through the heavens to the right hand of the Father. What if, after all, the old belief proves true that He returns to judgment after waiting for precisely the same period for which He had patiently endured their fathers' unbelief in the wilderness ! God is still living, and He is the same God. He Who sware in His wrath that the fathers should not enter into the rest of Canaan is the same in His anger, the same in His mercy. Exhort one another. In the wilderness God dealt with individuals. He does so still. See that there be no evil heart, which is unbelief, in *any one* of you at any time while the call, "To-day!" is sounded in your ears. For sin weakens the sense of individual guilt, and thus deceives men by hardening their hearts.* All that came out of Egypt provoked God to anger. But they

---

* Chap. ii. 13.

provoked Him, not in the mass, but one by one, and one by one, with palsied limbs,† they fell in the wilderness, as men fall exhausted on the march. Thus, for their persistent unbelief, God sware they should not enter into His rest—"His," for He kept the key still in His own hand. But persistent unbelief made them incapable of entering. If God were still willing to cut off for them the waters of Jordan, they *could* not * enter in because of unbelief.

3. Similarly, the promises of God are still in force. Indeed, the steadfastness of the threatenings involves the continuance of the promises, and the rejection of the promises ensures the fulfilment of every threatening. As much as this is expressed in the opening words of chap. iv.: "A promise being left to us, let us therefore fear."

To prove the identity of the promises under the two dispensations, the Apostle singles out one promise, which may be considered most significant of the national no less than the religious life of Israel. The Greek mind was ever on the alert for something new. Its character was movement. But the ideal of the Old Testament is rest. Christ came into touch with the people at once when He began His public ministry with an invitation to the weary and heavy-laden to come

---

* οὐκ ἠδυνήθησαν (iii. 19).   † τὰ κῶλα. Cf. chap. xii. 12.

unto Him, and with the promise that He would give them rest. Near the close of His ministry He explained and fulfilled the promise by giving to His disciples peace. The object of our author, in the difficult chapter now under consideration, is to show that the idea most characteristic of the old covenant finds its true and highest realisation in Christ. After the manner of St. Paul, who, in more than one passage, teaches that through the fall of Israel salvation is come unto the Gentiles, the writer of this Epistle also argues that the promise of rest still remains, because it was not fulfilled under the Old Testament in consequence of Israel's unbelief. The word of promise was a gospel * to them, as it is to us. But it did not profit them, because they did not assimilate † the promise by faith. Their history from the beginning consists of continued renewals of the promise on the part of God and persistent rejections on the part of Israel, ending in the hardening of their hearts. Every time the promise is renewed, it is presented in a higher and more spiritual form. Every rejection inevitably leads to grosser views and more hopeless unbelief. So entirely false is the fable of the Sibyl! God does not burn some of the leaves when His promises have been rejected, and come back with fewer offers at a higher

---

* εὐηγγελισμένοι (iv. 2).   † Reading συνκεκερασμένος.

price.   His method is to offer more and better on the same conditions.   But it is the nature of unbelief to cause the heart to wax gross, to blind the spiritual vision, until in the end the rich, spiritual promises of God and the earthly, dark unbelief of the sinner stand in extremest contrast.

At first the promise is presented in the negative form of rest from labour.   Even the Creator condescended thus to rest.   But what *such* rest can be to God it were vain for man to try to conceive.   We know that, as soon as the foundations of the world were laid and the work of creation was ended, God ceased from this form of activity.   But when this negative rest had been attained, it was far from realising God's idea of rest either for Himself or for man.   For, though these works of God, the material universe, were finished from the laying of the world's foundations to the crowning of the edifice,* God still speaks of another rest, and threatens to shut some men out for their un- belief.   Our Lord told the Pharisees, whose notion of the Sabbath was the negative one, that He desired His Sabbath rest to be like that of His Father, Who " worketh hitherto."   The Jewish Sabbath, it appears, therefore, is the most crude and elementary form of God's promised rest.

---

* Chap. iv. **3.**

The promise is next presented as the rest of Canaan.* This is a stage in advance in the development of the idea. It is not mere abstention from secular labour, and the consecration of inactivity. The rest now consists in the enjoyment of material prosperity, the proud consciousness of national power, the growth of a peculiar civilization, the rise of great men and eminent saints, and all this won by Israel under the leadership of their Jesus, who was in this respect a type of ours. But even in this second garden of Eden Israel did not attain unto God's rest. Worldliness became their snare.

But God still called to them by the mouth of the Psalmist, long after they had entered on the possession of Canaan. This only proves that the true rest was still unattained, and God's promise not yet fulfilled. The form which the rest of God now assumed is not expressly stated in our passage. But we have not far to go in search of it. The first Psalm, which is the introduction to all the Psalms, declares the blessedness of contemplation. The Sabbath is seldom mentioned by the Psalmist. Its place is taken by the sanctuary, in which rest of soul is found in meditating on God's law and beholding the Lord's beauty.† The call is at last urgent. "To-day!" It is the last invitation. It

---

* Chap. iv. 8.   † Ps. xxvii. 4.

lingers in the ears in ever fainter voice of prophet
after prophet, until the prophet's face turns towards
the east to announce the break of dawn and the coming
of the perfect rest in Jesus Christ. God's promise
was never fulfilled to Israel, because of their unbelief.
But shall their unbelief make the faithfulness of God
of none effect? God forbid. The gifts and calling of
God are without repentance. The promise that has
failed of fulfilment in the lower form must find its
accomplishment in the higher. Even a prayer is the
more heard for every delay. God's mill grinds slowly,
but for that reason grinds small. What is the inference? Surely it is that the Sabbath rest still
remains for the true people of God. This Sabbath
rest St. Paul prayed that the true Israel, who glory,
not in their circumcision, but in the Cross of our Lord
Jesus Christ, might receive: "*Peace* be upon them,
and mercy, and upon the Israel of God."*

The faithfulness of God to fulfil His promise in its
higher form is proved by His having accomplished it
in its more elementary forms to every one that believed. "For he that entered into God's rest did
actually rest from his works" †—that is to say, received
the blessings of the Sabbath—as truly as God rested
from the work of creation. The Apostle's practical

---

* Gal. vi. 16.   † Chap. iv. 10.

inference is couched in language almost paradoxical : "Let us *strive* to enter into God's *rest*"—not indeed into the rest of the Old Testament, but into the better rest which God now offers in His Son.

The oneness of the dispensations has been proved. They are one in their design, in their threatenings, in their promises.   If we seek the fundamental ground of this threefold unity, we shall find it in the fact that both dispensations are parts of a Divine revelation. God has spoken, and the word of God does not pass away.   "Think not," said our Lord, "that I came to destroy the Law or the prophets ; I came not to destroy, but to fulfil.   For verily I say unto you, Till heaven and earth pass away, one jot or one tittle shall in no wise pass away from the Law till all things be accomplished." *   On another occasion He says, "Heaven and earth shall pass away, but My words shall not pass away." †   These passages teach us that the words of God through Moses and in the Son are equally immutable.   Many features of the old covenant may be transient ; but, if it is a word of God, it abides in its essential nature through all changes.   For "the word of God is living," ‡ because He Who speaks the word is the living God.   It acts with mighty energy,§ like

---

* Matt. v. 17, 18.   ‡ Chap. iv. 12
† Matt. xxiv. 35.   § ἐνεργής.

the silent laws of nature, which destroy or save alive
according as men obey or disobey them.   It cuts like
a sword whetted on each side of the blade, piercing
through to the place where the natural life of the soul
divides * from, or passes into, the supernatural life of
the spirit.   For it is revelation that has made known
to man his possession of the spiritual faculty.   The
word "spirit" is used by heathen writers.   But in
their books it means only the air we breathe.   The
very conception of the spiritual is enshrined in the
bosom of God's word.   Revelation has separated
between the life of heathenism and the life of the
Church, between the natural man and the spiritual,
between the darkness that comprehended it not and the
children of the light who received it and thus became
children of God.   Further, the word of God pierces to
the joints that connect the natural and the supernatural.†   It does not ignore the former.   On the
contrary, it addresses itself to man's reason and conscience, in order to erect the supernatural upon nature.
Where reason stops short, the word of God appeals to
the supernatural faculty of faith ; and when conscience
grows blunt, the word makes conscience, like itself,
sharper than any two-edged sword.   Once more, the
word of God pierces to the marrow.‡   It reveals to

---

* μερισμοῦ.   † ἁρμῶν.   ‡ μυελῶν.

man the innermost meaning of his own nature and of
the supernatural planted within him.   The truest
morality and the highest spirituality are both the direct
product of God's revelation.

But all this is true in its practical application to
every man individually.   The power of the word of
God to create distinct dispensations and yet maintain
their fundamental unity, to distinguish between masses
of men and yet cause all the separate threads of human
history to converge and at last meet, is the same power
which judges the inmost thoughts and inmost purposes
of the heart.   These it surveys with critical judgment.*
If its eye is keen, its range of vision is also wide.
No created thing but is seen and manifest.   The surface is bared, and the depth within is opened up before
it.   As the upturned neck of the sacrificial beast lay
bare to the eye of God,† so are we exposed to the eye
of Him to Whom we have to give our account.‡

---

* κριτικός.   † τετραχηλισμένα (iv. 13).   ‡ ὁ λόγος.

THE GREAT HIGH-PRIEST.

" Having then a great High-priest, Who hath passed through the heavens, Jesus the Son of God, let us hold fast our confession. For we have not a high-priest that cannot be touched with the feeling of our infirmities ; but One that hath been in all points tempted like as we are, yet without sin. Let us therefore draw near with boldness unto the throne of grace, that we may receive mercy, and may find grace to help us in time of need. For every high-priest, being taken from among men, is appointed for men in things pertaining to God, that he may offer both gifts and sacrifices for sins : who can bear gently with the ignorant and erring, for that he himself also is compassed with infirmity ; and by reason thereof is bound, as for the people, so also for himself, to offer for sins. And no man taketh the honour unto himself, but when he is called of God, even as was Aaron. So Christ also glorified not Himself to be made a High-priest, but He that spake unto Him,

> Thou art My Son,
> This day have I begotten Thee :

as He saith also in another place,

> Thou art a Priest for ever
> After the order of Melchizedek.

Who in the days of His flesh, having offered up prayers and supplications with strong crying and tears unto Him that was able to save Him from death, and having been heard for His godly fear, though He was a Son, yet learned obedience by the things which He suffered ; and having been made perfect, He became unto all them that obey Him the Author of eternal salvation ; named of God a High-priest after the order of Melchizedek."—HEB. iv. 14—v. 10 (R.V.)

CHAPTER IV.

THE GREAT HIGH-PRIEST.

THE results already gained are such as these: that the Son, through Whom God has spoken unto us, is a greater Person than the angels; that Jesus, Whom the Apostle and the Hebrew Christians acknowledge to be Son of God, is the representative Man, endowed, as such, with kingly authority; that the Son of God became man in order that He might be constituted High-priest to make reconciliation for sin; and, finally, that all the purposes of God revealed in the Old Testament, though they have hitherto been accomplished but partially, will not fall to the ground, and will remain in higher forms under the Gospel.

The writer gathers these threads to a head in chap. iv. 14. The high-priest still remains. If we have the high-priest, we have all that is of lasting worth in the old covenant. For the idea of the covenant is reconciliation with God, and this is embodied and symbolised in the high-priest, inasmuch as he alone entered within the veil on the day of atonement. Having the high-priest in a greater Person, we have all the blessings of the covenant restored to us in a better form. The Epistle to the Hebrews is intended to encourage and comfort men who have lost their all. Judaism was in its death-throes. National independence had already ceased. When the Apostle was writing, the eagles were gathering around the carcase. But when all is lost, all is regained if we "have" the High-priest.

The secret of His abiding for ever is His own greatness. He is a *great* High-priest; for He has entered into the immediate presence of God, not through the Temple veil, but through the very heavens. In chap. viii. 1 the Apostle declares this to be the head and front of all he has said : "We have *such* an High-priest" as He must be "Who is set on the right hand of the throne of the Majesty in the heavens." He is a great High-priest because He is a Priest on a throne. As the representative Man, Jesus is crowned. His glory is kingly. But the glory bestowed on the Man as King has brought Him into the audience-chamber of God as High-priest. The kingship of Jesus, to Whom all creation is subjected, and Who sits above all creation, has made His priestly service effectual. His exaltation is much more than a reward for His redemptive sufferings. He entered the heaven of God as the sanctuary of which He is Minister. For if He were on earth, He would not be a Priest at all, seeing that He is not of the order of Aaron, to which the earthly priesthood belongs according to the Law.* But Christ is not entered into the holy place made with hands, but into the very heaven, now to be manifested before the face of God for us.† The Apostle has said that Christ is Son over the house of God. He is also High-priest over the house of God, having authority over it in virtue of His priesthood for it, and administering His priestly functions effectually through His kingship.‡

The entire structure of the Apostle's inferences rests on the twofold argument of the first two chapters. Jesus Christ is a great High-priest ; that is, King and High-priest in one, because He unites in His own person Son of God and Son of man.

One is tempted to find an intentional antithesis between the awe-inspiring description of the word of God in the previous verse and the tender language of the verse that follows. Is the word a living, ener‧ gising power ? The High-priest too is living and powerful, great and dwelling above the heavens. Does the word pierce to our innermost being ? The High-priest sympathises with our weaknesses, or, in the beautiful paraphrase of the English Version, "is touched with a feeling of our infirmities." Does the word

---

* Chap. viii. 4.   † Chap. ix. 24   ‡ Cf. chap. x. 21.

judge ? The High-priest can be equitable, inasmuch as He has been tempted like as we are tempted, and that without sin.*

On the last-mentioned point much might be said. He was tempted to sin, but withstood the temptation. He had true and complete humanity, and human nature, as such and alone, is capable of sin. Shall we, therefore, admit that Jesus was capable of sin ? But He was Son of God. Christ was Man, but not a human Person. He was a Divine Person, and there-fore absolutely and eternally incapable of sin ; for sin is the act and property of a person, not of a mere nature apart from the persons who have that nature. Having assumed humanity, the Divine person of the Son of God was truly tempted, like as we are. He felt the power of the temptation, which appealed in every case, not to a sinful lust, but to a sinless want and natural desire. But to have yielded to Satan and satisfied a sinless appetite at his suggestion would have been a sin. It would argue want of faith in God. Morcover, He strove against the tempter with the weapons of prayer and the word of God. He con-quered by His faith. Far from lessening the force of the trial, His being Son of God rendered His humanity capable of being tempted to the very utmost limit of

* Chap. iv. 15.

all temptation.   We dare not say that mere man would certainly have yielded to the sore trials that beset Jesus. But we do say that mere man would never have felt the temptation so keenly.   Neither did His Divine greatness lessen His sympathy.   Holy men have a wellspring of pity in their hearts, to which ordinary men are total strangers.   The infinitely holy Son of God had infinite pity.   These are the sources of His power to succour the tempted,—the reality of His temptations as He was Son of man, the intensity of them as He was Son of God, and the compassion of One Who was both Son of God and Son of man.

Our author is wont to break off suddenly and intersperse his arguments with affectionate words of exhortation.   He does so here.   It is still the same urgent command : Do not let go the anchor.   Hold fast your profession of Christ as Son of God and Son of man, as Priest and King.   Let us draw nearer, and that boldly, unto this great High-priest, Who is enthroned on the mercy-seat, that we may obtain the pity which, in our sense of utter helplessness, we seek, and *find* more than we seek or hope for, even His grace to help us.   Only linger not till it be too late.   His aid must be sought in time.*   " To-day " is still the call.

Pity and helping grace, sympathy and authority—

---

* εὔκαιρον (iv. 16),

in these two excellences all the qualifications of a
high-priest are comprised. It was so under the old
covenant. Every high-priest was taken from among
men that he might sympathise, and was appointed by
God that he might have authority to act on behalf
of men.

1. The high-priest under the Law is himself beset
by the infirmities of sinful human nature, the infirmities at least for which alone the Law provides
a sacrifice, sins of ignorance and inadvertence.*
Thus only can he form a fair and equitable judgment † when men go astray. The thought wears the
appearance of novelty. No use is apparently made of
it in the Old Testament. The notion of the high-
priest's Divine appointment overshadowed that of his
human sympathy. His sinfulness is acknowledged,
and Aaron is commanded to offer sacrifice for himself
and for the sins of the people.‡ But the author of
this Epistle states the reason why a sinful man was
made high-priest. He has told us that the Law was
given through angels. But no angel interposed as
high-priest between the sinner and God. Sympathy
would be wanting to the angel. But the very infirmity
that gave the high-priest his power of sympathy made
sacrifice necessary for the high-priest himself. This

---

* Chap. v. 1, 2,   † μετριοπαθεῖν.   ‡ Lev. xvi. 6.

was the fatal defect.   How can he bestow forgiveness who must seek the like forgiveness ?

In the case of the great High-priest, Jesus the Son of God, the end must be sought in another way.   He is not so taken from the stock of humanity as to be stained with sin.   He is not one of many men, any one of whom might have been chosen.   On the contrary, He is holy, innocent, stainless, separated in character and position before God from the sinners around Him.*   He has no need to offer sacrifice for any sin of His own, but only for the sins of the people ; and this He did once for all when He offered up Himself.   For the Law makes mere men, beset with sinful infirmity, priests ; but the word of the oath makes the Son Priest, Who has been perfected for His office for ever.†   In this respect He bears no resemblance to Aaron.   Yet God did not leave His people without a type of Jesus in this complete separateness.   The Psalmist speaks of Him as a Priest after the order of Melchizedek, and concerning Christ as the Melchizedek Priest the Apostle has more to say hereafter.‡

The question returns, How, then, can the Son of God sympathise with sinful man ?   He can sympathise with our sinless infirmities because He is true Man. But that He, the sinless One, may be able to sympa-

---

* Chap. vii. 26.   † Chap. vii. 28.   ‡ Chap. v. 10, 11.

thise with sinful infirmities, He must be made sin
for us and face death as a sin-offering. The High-
priest Himself becomes the sacrifice which He offers.
Special trials beset Him. His life on earth is pre-
eminently "days of the flesh," * so despised is He,
a very Man of sorrows. When He could not
acquire the power of sympathy by offering atonement
for Himself, because He needed it not, He *offered*
prayers and supplications with a strong cry and
tears to Him Who was able to save Him out of
death. But why the strong cries and bitter weeping?
Can we suppose for a moment that He was only afraid
of physical pain? Or did He dread the shame of the
Cross? Our author elsewhere says that He despised it.
Shall we say that Jesus Christ had less moral courage
than Socrates or His own martyr-servant, St. Ignatius?
At the same time, let us confine ourselves strictly to
the words of Scripture, lest by any gloss of our own
we ascribe to Christ's death what is required by the
exigencies of a ready-made theory. "Being in an
agony, He prayed more earnestly; and His sweat
became as it were great drops of blood falling down
upon the ground." † Is this the attitude of a martyr?
The Apostle himself explains it. "Though He was

---

* Chap. v. 7.

† Luke xxii. 44. The genuineness of the verse is not quite certain.

a Son," to Whom obedience to His Father's command
that He should lay down His life was natural and
joyful, yet He learned His obedience, special and
peculiar as it was, by the things which He suffered.*
He was perfecting Himself to be our High-priest. By
these acts of priestly offering He was rendering Himself fit to be the sacrifice offered.   Because there was
in His prayers and supplications, in His crying and
weeping, this element of entire self-surrender to His
Father's will, which is the truest piety,† His prayers
were heard. He prayed to be delivered out of His
death. He prayed for the glory which He had with
His Father before the world was. At the same time.
He piously resigned Himself to die as a sacrifice, and
left it to God to decide whether He would raise Him
from death or leave His soul in Hades. Because of
this perfect self-abnegation, His sacrifice was complete ;
and, on the other hand, because of the same entire
self-denial, God did deliver Him out of death and made
Him an eternal Priest. His prayers were not only
heard, but became the foundation and beginning of His
priestly intercession on behalf of others.

2. The second essential qualification of a high-
priest was authority to act for men in things pertaining
to God, and in His name to absolve the penitent

---

* Cf. John x. 18.   † ἀπὸ τῆς εὐλαβείας (v. 7).

sinner. Prayer was free to all God's people and even
to the stranger that came out of a far country for the
sake of the God of Israel's name. But guilt, by its
very nature, involves the need, not merely of reconciling the sinner, but primarily of reconciling God. Hence
the necessity of a Divine appointment. For how can
man bring his sacrifice to God or know that God has
accepted it unless God Himself appoints the mediator
and through him pronounces the sinner absolved?
It is true, if man only is to be reconciled, a Divinely
appointed prophet will be enough, who will declare
God's fatherly love and so remove the sinner's unbelief
and slay his enmity. But the Epistle to the Hebrews
teaches that God appoints a high-priest. This of
itself is fatal to the theory that God needs not to be
reconciled. In the sense of having this Divine authori-
zation, the priestly office is here said to be an honour,
which no man takes upon himself, but accepts when
called thereunto by God.*

How does this apply to the great High-priest Who
has passed through the heavens? He also glorified
not Himself to become High-priest. The Apostle has
changed the word.† To Aaron it was an honour to be
high-priest. He was authorized to act for God and for
men. But to Christ it was more than an honour, more

---

* Chap. v. 4. † τιμήν (v. 4) ; ἐδόξασεν (v. 5).

than an external authority conferred upon Him. It
was part of the glory inseparable from His Sonship.
He Who said to Him, "Thou art My Son," made Him
thereby potentially High-priest. His office springs
from His personality, and is not, as in the case of
Aaron, a prerogative superadded. The author has
cited the second Psalm in a previous passage * to prove
the kingly greatness of the Son, and here again he
cites the same words to describe His priestly character.
His priesthood is not "from men," and, therefore, does
not pass away from Him to others; and this eternal,
independent priesthood of Christ is typified in the king-
priest Melchizedek. Before He began to act in His
priestly office God said to Him, "Thou art a Priest for
ever after the order of Melchizedek." When He has
been perfected and learned His obedience † by the
things which He suffered, God still addresses Him as
a High-priest according to the order of Melchizedek.

---

* Chap. i. 5.   † τὴν ὑπακοήν (v. 8).

THE IMPOSSIBILITY OF RENEWAL.

"Of Whom we have many things to say, and hard of interpretation, seeing ye are become dull of hearing. For when by reason of the time ye ought to be teachers, ye have need again that some one teach you the rudiments of the first principles of the oracles of God ; and are become such as have need of milk, and not of solid food. For every one that partaketh of milk is without experience of the word of righteousness ; for he is a babe. But solid food is for full-grown men, even those who by reason of use have their senses exercised to discern good and evil. Wherefore let us cease to speak of the first principles of Christ, and press on unto perfection ; not laying again a foundation of repentance from dead works, and of faith toward God, of the teaching of baptisms, and of laying on of hands, and of resurrection of the dead, and of eternal judgment. And this will we do, if God permit. For as touching those who were once enlightened and tasted of the heavenly gift, and were made partakers of the Holy Ghost, and tasted the good word of God, and the powers of the age to come, and then fell away, it is impossible to renew them again unto repentance ; seeing they crucify to themselves the Son of God afresh, and put Him to an open shame. For the land which hath drunk the rain that cometh oft upon it, and bringeth forth herbs meet for them for whose sake it is also tilled, receiveth blessing from God : but if it beareth thorns and thistles, it is rejected and nigh unto a curse ; whose end is to be burned."—HEB. v. 11—vi. 8 (R.V.).

CHAPTER V.

THE IMPOSSIBILITY OF RENEWAL.

IN one of the greatest and most strange of human books the argument is sometimes said "to veil itself," and the sustained image of a man battling with the waves betrays the writer's hesitancy. When he has surmounted the first wave, he dreads the second. When he has escaped out of the second, he fears to take another step, lest the third wave may overwhelm him. The writer of the Epistle to the Hebrews has proved that Christ is Priest-King. But before he starts anew, he warns his readers that whoever will venture on must be prepared to hear a hard saying, which he himself will find difficult to interpret and few will receive. Hitherto he has only shown that whatever of lasting worth was contained in the old covenant remains and is exalted in Christ. Even this truth is an advance on the mere rudiments of Christian doctrine. But what if he attempts to prove that the covenant which God made with their fathers has waxed old and must vanish away to make room for a new and better one ? For his part, he is eager to ascend to these higher truths. He has yet much to teach about Christ in the power of His heavenly life.* But his readers are dull of hearing and inexperienced in the word of right-eousness.

The commentators are much divided and exercised on the question whether the Apostle means that the argument should advance or that his readers ought to make progress in spiritual character.† In a way he surely means both. What gives point to the whole section now to be considered is the connection between development of doctrine and a corresponding develop-ment of the moral nature. "For the time ye ought to be teachers." ‡ They ought to have been teachers of the elementary truths, in consequence of having dis-covered the higher truths for themselves, under the guidance of God's Spirit. It ought to have been unnecessary for the Apostle to explain them. At this time the "teachers" in the Church had probably con-solidated into a class formally set apart, but had not yet fallen to the second place, as compared with the "prophets," which they occupy in the "Teaching of the Twelve Apostles." A long time had elapsed since the Church of Jerusalem, with the Apostles and elders, had sat in judgment on the question submitted to their

---

* Chap. v. 11. † Chap. vi. 1. ‡ Chap. v. 12.

decision by such men as Peter, Barnabas, Paul, and
James.* Since then the Hebrew Christians had de-
generated, and now needed somebody—it mattered
little who it might be †—to teach them the alphabet ‡
of Christian doctrine.

Philo had already emphasised the distinction between
the child in knowledge and the man of full age and
mature judgment. St. Paul had said more than once
that such a distinction holds among Christians. Many
are carnal; some are spiritual. In his writings the
difference is not an external one, nor is the line between
the two classes broad and clear. The one shades into
the other. But, though we may not be able to deter-
mine where the one begins and the other ends, both
are tendencies, and move in opposite directions. In
the Epistle to the Hebrews the distinction resembles
the old doctrine of habit taught by Aristotle. Our
organs of sense are trained by use to distinguish forms
and colours. In like manner, there are inner organs
of the spirit,§ which distinguish good from evil, not
by mathematical demonstration, but by long-continued
exercise ‖ in hating evil and in loving holiness. The
growth of this spiritual sense is connected by our
author with the power to understand the higher doctrine. He only who discerns, by force of spiritual

---

* Acts xv.   † τινά (v. 12).   ‡ στοιχεῖα.   § αἰσθητήρια.
‖ γεγυμνασμένα.

insight, what is good and what is evil, can also understand spiritual truths. The difference between good
and evil is not identical with "the word of righteousness." But the moral elevation of character that
clearly discerns the former is the condition of understanding also the latter.

"Wherefore"—that is, inasmuch as solid food is for
full-grown men—"let us have done * with the elementary doctrines, and permit ourselves to be borne
strongly onwards † towards full growth of spiritual
character." ‡ The Apostle has just said that his readers
needed some one to teach them the rudiments. We
should have expected him, therefore, to take it in hand.
But he reminds them that the defect lies deeper than
intellectual error. The remedy is not mere teaching,
but spiritual growth. Apart from moral progress there
can be no revelation of new truths. Ever-recurring
efforts to lay the foundation of individual piety will
result only in an apprehension of what we may de-
signate personal and subjective doctrines.

The Apostle particularises. Repentance towards
God and faith in God are the initial graces.§ For
without sorrow for sin and trust in God's mercy God's
revelation of Himself in His Son will not be deemed
worthy of all acceptation. If this is so, the doctrines

---

* ἀφέντες (vi. 1).　† φερώμεθα.　‡ τελειότητα.　§ θεμέλιον.

suitable to the initial stage of the Christian life will be—
(1) the doctrine of baptisms and of laying on of hands,
and (2) the doctrine of the resurrection of the dead
and of eternal judgment. Repentance and faith accept
the gospel of forgiveness, which is symbolised in
baptism, and of absolution, symbolised in the laying on
of hands. Again, repentance and faith realise the
future life and the final award; the beginning of piety
reaching forth a hand, as runners do, as if to grasp the
furthest goal before it touches the intermediate points.
Yet every intermediate truth, when apprehended,
throws new light on the soul's eschatology. In like
manner civilization began with contemplation of the
stars, long before it descended to chemical analysis,
but at last it applies its chemistry to make discoveries
in the stars.

This, then, is the initial stage in the Christian
character,—repentance and faith; and these are the
initial doctrines,—baptism, absolution, resurrection,
and judgment. How may they be described? They all
centre in the individual believer. They have all to do
with the fact of his sin. One question, and one only,
presses for an answer. It is, "What must I do to be
saved?" One result, and one only, flows from the
salvation obtained. It is the final acquittal of the
sinner at the last day. God is known only as the
merciful Saviour and the holy Judge. The whole of

the believer's personal existence hovers in mid-air
between two points : repentance at some moment in the
past and judgment at the end of the world. Works
are " dead," and the reason why is that they have no
saving power. There is here no thought of life as a
complete thing or as a series of possibilities that ever
spring into actuality, no thought of the individual as
being part of a greater whole. The Church exists for
the sake of the believer, not the believer for the sake
of the Church. Even Christ Himself is nothing more
to him than his Saviour, Who by an atoning death
paid his debt. The Apostle would rise to higher truths
concerning Christ in the power of His heavenly life.
This is the truth which the story of Melchizedek will
teach to such as are sufficiently advanced in spirituality
to understand its meaning.

But, before he faces the rolling wave, the Apostle
tells his readers why it is that, in reference to Christian
doctrine, character is the necessary condition of intelligence. It is so for two reasons.

First, the word spoken by God in His Son has for
its primary object, not speculation, but "righteousness." * Theology is essentially a practical, not a
merely theoretical, science. Its purpose is to create
righteous men ; that is, to produce a certain character.

---

* Chap. v. 13.

When produced, this lofty character is sustained by the truths of the Gospel as by a spiritual "food," milk or strong meat. Christianity is the art of holy living, and the art is mastered only as every other art is learned: by practice or experience. But experience will suggest rules, and rules will lead to principles. The art itself creates a faculty to transform it into a science. Religion will produce a theology. The doctrine will be understood only by the possessor of that goodness to which it has itself given birth.

Second, the Apostle introduces the personal action of God into the question. Understanding of the higher truths is God's blessing on goodness,* and destruction of the faculty of spiritual discernment is His way of punishing moral depravity.† This is the general sense and purport of an extremely difficult passage. The threatened billow is still far away. But before it rolls over us, we seem to be already submerged under the waves. Our only hope lies in the Apostle's illustration of the earth that bears here thorns and there good grain.

Expositors go quite astray when they explain the simile as if it were intended to describe the effect on moral character of rightly or wrongly using our faculty of knowledge. The meaning is the reverse. The

---

* Chap. vi. 7.   † Chap. v 8.

Apostle is showing the effect of character on our power to understand truth. Neither soil is barren. Both lands drink in the rain that often comes upon them. But the fatness of the one field brings forth thorns and thistles, and this can only mean that the man's vigour of soul is itself an occasion of moral evil. The richness of the other land produces plants fit for use by men, who are the sole reason for its tillage.* This, again, must mean that, in the case of some men, God blesses that natural strength which itself is neither good nor evil, and it becomes a source of goodness. We come now to the result in each case. The soil that brings forth useful herbs has its share of the Creator's first blessing. What the blessing consists in we are not here told, and it is not necessary to pursue this side of the illustration further. But the other soil, which gives its natural strength to the production of noxious weeds, falls under the Creator's primal curse and is nigh unto burning. The point of the parable evidently is that God blesses the one, that God destroys the other. In both cases the Apostle recognises the Divine action, carrying into effect a Divine threat and a Divine promise.

Let us see how the simile is applied. The terrible word "impossible" might indeed have been pronounced,

---

* δι᾿ οὕς.

with some qualification, over a man who had fallen under the power of evil habits. For God sets His seal to the verdict of our moral nature. To such a man the only escape is through the strait gate of repentance. But here we have much more than the ordinary evil habits of men, such as covetousness, hypocrisy, carnal imaginations, cruelty. The Apostle is thinking throughout of God's revelation in His Son. He refers to the righteous anger of God against those who persistently despise the Son. In the second chapter * he has asked how men who neglect the salvation spoken through the Lord can hope to shun God's anger. Here he declares the same truth in a stronger form. How shall they escape His wrath who crucify afresh the Son and put Him to an open shame ? Such men God will punish by hardening their hearts, so that they cannot even repent. The initial grace becomes impossible.

The four parts of the simile and of the application correspond.

First, drinking in the rain that often comes upon the land corresponds to being once enlightened, tasting of the heavenly gift, being made partakers of the Holy Ghost, and tasting the good word of God and the powers of the world to come. The rain descends on all the land and gives it its natural richness. The

---

* Chap. ii. 3.

question whether the Apostle speaks of converted or unconverted men is entirely beside the purpose, and may safely be relegated to the limbo of misapplied interpretations. No doubt the controversy between Calvinists and Arminians concerning final perseverance and the possibility of a fall from a state of grace is itself vastly important. But tne question whether the gifts mentioned are bestowed on an unconverted man is of no importance to the right apprehension of the Apostle's meaning. We must be forgiven for thinking he had it not in his mind. It is more to the purpose to remind ourselves that all these excellences are regarded by the Apostle as gifts of God, like the oft-descending rain, not as moral qualities in men. He mentions the one enlightenment produced by the one revelation of God in His Son. It may be compared to the opening of blind eyes or the startled waking of the soul by a great idea. To taste the heavenly gift is to make trial of the new truth. To be made partakers of the Holy Ghost is to be moved by a supernatural en-lightening influence. To taste the good word of God is to discern the moral beauty of the revelation. To taste the powers of the world to come is to participate in the gifts of power which the Spirit divides to each one severally even as He will. All these things have an intellectual quality. Faith in Christ and love to God are purposely excluded. The Apostle brings

together various phases of our spiritual intelligence,—
the gift of illumination, which we sometimes call genius,
sometimes culture, sometimes insight, the faculty that
ought to apprehend Christ and welcome the revelation
in the Son.   If these high gifts are used to scoff at the
Son of God, and that with the persistence that can
spring only from the pride and self-righteousness of
unbelief, renewal is impossible.

Second, the negative result of not bringing forth any
useful herbs corresponds to falling away.*   God has
bestowed His gift of enlightenment, but there is no
response of heart and will.   The soul does not lay
hold, but drifts away.

Third, the positive result of bearing thorns and
thistles corresponds to crucifying to themselves the Son
of God afresh and putting Him to an open shame.
The gifts of God have been abused, and the contrary
of what He, in His care for men, intended the earth
to produce, is the result.   The Divine gift of spiritual
enlightenment has been itself turned into a very genius
of cynical mockery.   The Son of God has already
been once crucified amid the awful scenes of Gethsemane and Calvary.   The agony and bloody sweat,
the cry of infinite loneliness on the Cross, the tender
compassion of the dying Jesus, the power of His resur-

---

* παραπεσόντας (vi. 5).   Cf. παραρυῶμεν (ii 1)

rection—all this is past. One bitterness yet remains.
Men use God's own gift of spiritual illumination to
crucify the Son afresh. But they crucify Him only
for themselves.* When the sneer has died away on
the scoffer's lips, nothing is left. No result has been
achieved in the moral world. When Christ was
crucified on Calvary, His death changed for ever the
relations of God and men. When He is crucified in
the reproach of His enemies, nothing has been accomplished outside the scoffer's little world of vanity and
pride.

Fourth, to be nigh unto a curse and to be given in
the end to be burned corresponds to the impossibility
of renewal. The illustration requires us to distinguish
between " falling away " and " crucifying the Son of
God afresh and putting Him to an open shame."† The
land is doomed to be burned because it bears thorns
and thistles. God renders men incapable of repentance, not because they have fallen away once or more
than once, but because they scoff at the Son, through
Whom God has spoken unto us. The terrible impos-

---

* ἑαυτοῖς.

† Apart from the exigencies of the illustration, the change from the
aorist participle to the present participles tells in the same way. It
is extremely harsh to consider ἀνασταυροῦντας and παραδειγματίζοντας
to be explanatory of παραπεσόντας. The former must be rendered
hypothetically : " They cannot be renewed after falling away if they
persist in crucifying,' etc.

sibility of renewal here threatened applies, not to apostasy (as the early Church maintained) nor to the lapsed (as the Novatianists held),* but to apostasy combined with a cynical, scoffing temper that persists in treading the Son of God under foot. Apostasy resembles the sin against the Son of man ; cynicism in reference to the Son of man comes very near the sin against the Holy Ghost. This sin is not forgiven, because it hardens the heart and makes repentance impossible. It hardens the heart, because God is jealous of His Son's honour, and punishes the scoffer with the utter destruction of the spiritual faculty and with absolute inability to recover it. This is not the mere force of habit. It is God's retribution, and the Apostle mentions it here because the text of the whole Epistle is that God has spoken unto us in His Son.

But the Hebrew Christians have not come to this.† The Apostle is persuaded better things of them, and things that are nigh, not unto a curse, but unto ultimate salvation. Yet they are not free from the danger. If we may appropriate the language of an eminent historian, "the worship of wealth, grandeur,

---

* The apostates, or deserters, were not identical with the lapsed, who fell away from fear of martyrdom. Novatian refused to restore either to Church privileges. The Church restored the latter, but not the former. Cf. Cyprian, Ep. lv. *ad fin.*

† Chap. vi. 9.

and dominion blinded the Jews to the form of spiritual godliness ; the rejection of the Saviour and the deification of Herod were parallel manifestations of the same engrossing delusion."* That the Christian Hebrews may not fall under the curse impending over their race, the Apostle urges them to press on unto full growth of character. And this he and they will do— he ranks himself among them, and ventures to make reply in their name. But He must add an "if God permit." For there are men whom God will not permit to advance a jot higher. Because they have abused His great gift of illumination to scoff at the greater gift of the Son, they are doomed to forfeit possession of both. The only doomed man is the cynic.

* Dean Merivale, *Romans under the Empire*, chap. lix.

THE IMPOSSIBILITY OF FAILURE.

"But, beloved, we are persuaded better things of you, and things that accompany salvation, though we thus speak: for God is not unrighteous to forget your work and the love which ye showed toward His name, in that ye ministered unto the saints, and still do minister. And we desire that each one of you may show the same diligence unto the fulness of hope even to the end: that ye be not sluggish, but imitators of them who through faith and patience inherit the promises. For when God made promise to Abraham, since He could swear by none greater, He sware by Himself, saying, Surely blessing I will bless thee, and multiplying I will multiply thee. And thus, having patiently endured, he obtained the promise. For men swear by the greater: and in every dispute of theirs the oath is final for confirmation. Wherein God, being minded to show more abundantly unto the heirs of the promise the immutability of His counsel, interposed with an oath: that by two immutable things, in which it is impossible for God to lie, we may have a strong encouragement, who have fled for refuge to lay hold of the hope set before us; which we have as an anchor of the soul, a hope both sure and steadfast and entering into that which is within the veil; whither as a Forerunner Jesus entered for us, having become a High-priest for ever after the order of Melchizedek."—HEB. vi. 9—20 (R.V.).

CHAPTER VI.

THE IMPOSSIBILITY OF FAILURE.

SOLEMN warning is followed by words of affectionate encouragement. Impossibility of renewal is not the only impossibility within the compass of the Gospel.* Over against the descent to perdition, hope of the better things grasps salvation with the one hand and the climbing pilgrim with the other, and makes his failure to reach the summit impossible. Both impossibilities have their source in God's justice. He is not unjust to forget the deed of love shown towards His name, when the only-begotten Son ministered to men and still ministers. Contempt of this love God will punish. Neither is He unjust to forget the love that ministered to His poor saints in days of persecution, when the Hebrew Christians became partakers with their fellow-believers in their reproaches and tribulations, showed pity towards their brethren in prisons, and took joyfully the spoiling of their goods.† The stream of brotherly kindness was still flowing. This

---

* Compare chap. vi. 4 and chap. vi. 18.　　† Chap. x. 34.

love God rewards. But the Apostle desires them **to** show, not only faithfulness in ministering to the **saints,** but also Christian earnestness generally,* until they attain the full assurance of hope. The older expositors understand the words to express the Apostle's wish that his readers should continue to minister to the saints. But Calvin's view has, especially since the time of Bengel, been generally accepted : that the Apostle urges his readers to be as diligent in seeking the full assurance of hope as they are in ministering to the poor. This is most probably the meaning, but with the addition that he speaks of " earnestness " generally not merely of active diligence. Their religion was too narrow in range. Care for the poor has sometimes been the piety of sluggish despondency and bigotry. But spiritual earnestness is the moral discipline that works hope, a hope that makes not ashamed, but leads men on to an assured confidence that the promise of God will be fulfilled, though now black clouds over-spread their sky.

An incentive to faith and endurance will be found in the example of all inheritors of God's promise.† The Apostle is on the verge of anticipating the splendid record of the eleventh chapter. But he arrests himself, partly because, at the present stage of his argument,

---

* σπουδήν (vi. 11).   † Chap. vi. 13.

he can speak of faith only as the deep fountain of endurance. He cannot now describe it as the realisation and the proof of things unseen.* He wishes, moreover, to dwell on the oath made by God to Abraham. Even this, if not an anticipation of what is still to come, is at least a preparation of the reader for the distinction hereafter effectively handled between the high-priest made without an oath and the High-priest made with an oath. But, in the present section, the emphatic notion is that the promise made to Abraham is the same promise which the Apostle and his brethren wait to see fulfilled, and that the confirmation of the promise by oath to Abraham is still in force for their strong encouragement. It is true that Abraham received the fulfilment of the promise in his lifetime, but only in a lower form. The promise, like the Sabbath rest, has become more and still more elevated, profound, spiritual, with the long delay of God to make it good. It is equally true that the saints under the Old Testament received not the fulfilment of the promise in its highest meaning, and were not perfected apart from believers of after-ages.† God's words never grow obsolete. They are never left behind by the Church. If they seem to pass away, they return laden with still choicer fruit. The coursing moon

---

* Chap. xi. 1.   † Chap. xi. 40.

in the high heavens is never outstripped by the belated traveller. The hope of the Gospel is ever set before us. God swears to Abraham in the spring-time of the world that *we*, on whom the ends of the ages have come, may have a strong incentive to press onwards.

But, if the oath of God to Abraham is to inspire us with new courage, we must resemble Abraham in the eager earnestness and calm endurance of his faith. The passage has often been treated as if the oath had been intended to meet the weakness of faith. But unbelief is logician enough to argue that God's word is as good as His bond ; yea, that we have no knowledge of His oath except from His word. The Apostle refers to the greatest instance of faith ever shown even by Abraham, when he withheld not his son, his beloved son, on Moriah. The oath was made to him by God, not before he gave up Isaac, in order to encourage his weakness, but when he had done it, as a reward of his strength. Philo's fine sentence, which indeed the sacred writer partly borrows, is intended to teach the same lesson : that, while disappointments are heaped on sense, an endless abundance of good things has been given to the earnest soul and the perfect man.* It is to Abraham when he has achieved his supreme victory of faith that God vouchsafes to make

---

* *SS. Legg. Alleg.*, iii., p. 98 (vol. i., p. 127, Mang.). With Philo's τῇ σπουδαίᾳ ψυχῇ compare the Apostle's σπουδήν (chap. v. 11).

oath that He will fulfil His promise.   This gives us
the clue to the purport of the words.   Up to this final
test of Abraham's faith God's promise is, so to speak,
conditional.   It will be fulfilled if Abraham will believe.
Now at length the promise is given unconditionally.
Abraham has gone triumphantly through every trial.
He has not withheld his son.   So great is his faith
that God can now confirm His promise with a positive
declaration, which transforms a promise made to a man
into a prediction that binds Himself.   Or shall we
retract the expression that the promise is now given
unconditionally ?   The condition is transferred from
the faith of Abraham to the faithfulness of God.   In
this lies the oath.   God pledges His own existence on
the fulfilment of His promise.   He says no longer, " If
thou canst believe," but " As true as I live."   Speaking
humanly, unbelief on the part of Abraham would have
made the promise of God of none effect; for it was
conditional on Abraham's faith.   But the oath has
raised the promise above being affected by the unbelief
of some, and itself includes the faith of some.   St. Paul
can now ask, " What if some did not believe ?   Shall
their unbelief make the *faith*" (no longer merely the
promise) " of God without effect ? " *   Our author also
can speak of two immutable things, in which it was

---

* Rom. iii. 3.

impossible for God to lie.   The one is the promise, the immutability of which means only that God, on His part, does not retract, but casts on men the blame if the promise is not fulfilled.   The other is the oath, in which God takes the matter into His own hands and puts the certainty of His fulfilling the promise to rest on His own eternal being.

The Apostle is careful to point out the wide and essential difference between the oath of God and the oaths of men.   " For men swear by the greater ; " that is, they call upon God, as the Almighty, to destroy them if they are uttering what is false.   They imprecate a curse upon themselves.   If they have sworn to a falsehood, and if the imprecation falls on their heads, they perish, and the matter ends.   And yet an oath decides all disputes between man and man.*   Though they appeal to an Omnipotence that often turns a deaf ear to their prayer against themselves ; though, if the Almighty were to fling retribution on them, the wheels of nature would whirl as merrily as before ; though, if their false swearing were to cause the heavens to fall, the men would still exist and continue to be men ; —yet, for all this, they accept an oath as final settlement.   They are compelled to come to terms ; for they are at their wits' end.   But it is very different with the

---

* Chap. vi. 16.

oath of God.   When He swears by Himself, He appeals, not to His omnipotence, but to His truthfulness.   If any jot or tittle of God's promise fails to the feeblest child that trusts Him, God ceases to be.   He has been annihilated, not by an act of power, but by a lie.

We have said that the oath met, not the weakness, but the strength, of Abraham's faith.   If so, why was it given him ?

First, it simplified his faith.   It removed all tendency to morbid introspection and filled his spirit with a peaceful reliance on God's faithfulness.   He had no more need to try himself whether he was in the faith. Anxious effort and painful struggle were over.   Faith was now the very life of his soul.   He could leave his concerns to God, and wait.   This is the thought expressed in the word "enduring."

Second, it was a new revelation of God to him, and thus elevated his spiritual nature.   The moral character of the Most High, rather than His natural attribute of omnipotence, became the resting-place of his spirit.   Even the joy of God's heart was made known and communicated to his.   God was pleased with Abraham's final victory over unbelief, and wished to show him more abundantly * His counsel and the immutability of it.   " The secret of the Lord is with

---

* περισσότερον.

them that fear Him, and He will show them His covenant." *

Third, it was intended also for our encouragement. It is strange, but true, that the promises of God are confirmed to us by the victorious faith of a nomad chief from Ur of the Chaldees, who, in the morning of the world's history, withheld not his son. After all, we are not disconnected units. God only can trace the countless threads of influence. Abraham's strong faith evoked the oath that now sustains the weakness of ours. Because he believed so well, the promise comes to us with all the sanction of God's own truth and unchangeableness. The oath made to Abraham was linked with a still more ancient, even an eternal, oath, made to the Son, constituting Him Priest for ever after the order of Melchizedek. The priesthood of Melchizedek is said by the Apostle to be a type of the priesthood founded on an oath. It was becoming that the man who acknowledged the priesthood of Melchizedek and received its blessing should have that blessing fulfilled to him in the confirmation by oath of God's promise. Thus the promises that have been fulfilled through the eternal priesthood of the true Melchizedek are confirmed to us by an oath made to him who acknowledged that priesthood in the typical Melchizedek.

---

* Ps. xxiv. 14.

Yet, notwithstanding these vital points of contact, Abraham and the Hebrew Christians are in some respects very unlike.   They have left his serene and contemplative life far behind.   The souls of men are stirred with dread of the threatened end of all things. Abraham had no need to flee for refuge from an impending wrath.   His religion even was not a fleeing from any wrath to come, but a yearning for a better fatherland.   He never heard the midnight cry of Maranatha, but longed to be gathered to his fathers. If any similitude to the Christian's fleeing from the wrath to come must be sought in ancient days, it will be found in the history of Lot, not of Abraham. Whether the Apostle's thoughts rested for a moment on Lot's flight from Sodom, it is impossible to say. His mind is moving so rapidly that one illustration after another flits before his eye.   The notion of Abraham's strong faith, reaching out a hand to the strong grasp of God's oath, reminds him of men fleeing for refuge, perhaps into a sanctuary, and laying hold of the horns of the altar, with a reminiscence of the Baptist's taunting question, "Who warned you to flee from the wrath to come?" and a side glance at the approaching destruction of the holy city, if indeed the catastrophe had not already befallen the doomed people.   The thought suggests another illustration. Our hope is an anchor cast into the deep sea.   The anchor is sure and steadfast—" sure," for, like Abraham's faith, it will neither break nor bend; " steadfast," for, like Abraham's faith again, it bites the eternal rock of the oath. Still another metaphor lends itself. The deep sea is above all heavens in the sanctuary within the veil, and the rock is Jesus, Who has entered into the holiest place as our High-priest. Yet another thought. Jesus is not only High-priest, but also Captain, of the redeemed host, leading us on, and opening the way for us to enter after Him into the sanctuary of the promised land.

Thus, with the help of metaphor heaped on metaphor in the fearless confusion delightful to conscious strength and gladness, the Apostle has at last come to the great conception of Christ in the sanctuary of heaven. He has hesitated long to plunge into the wave; and even now he will not at once lift the veil from the argument. The allegory of Melchizedek must prepare us for it.

THE ALLEGORY OF MELCHIZEDEK.

HEBREWS vii. 1—28 (R.V.).

'For this Melchizedek, King of Salem, priest of God Most High, who met Abraham returning from the slaughter of the kings, and blessed him, to whom also Abraham divided a tenth part of all (being first, by interpretation, King of righteousness, and then also King of Salem, which is, King of peace; without father, without mother, without genealogy, having neither beginning of days nor end of life, but made like unto the Son of God), abideth a priest continually. Now consider how great this man was, unto whom Abraham, the patriarch, gave a tenth out of the chief spoils. And they indeed of the sons of Levi that receive the priest's office have commandment to take tithes of the people according to the law, that is, of their brethren, though these have come out of the loins of Abraham : but he whose genealogy is not counted from them hath taken tithes of Abraham, and hath blessed him that hath the promises. But without any dispute the less is blessed of the better. And here men that die receive tithes ; but there one, of whom it is witnessed that he liveth. And, so to say, through Abraham even Levi, who receiveth tithes, hath paid tithes; for he was yet in the loins of his father, when Melchizedek met him. Now if there was perfection through the Levitical priesthood (for under it hath the people received the Law), what further need was there that another Priest should arise after the order of Melchizedek, and not be reckoned after the order of Aaron? For the priesthood being changed, there is made of necessity a change also of the law. For He of Whom these things are said belongeth to another tribe, from which no man hath given attendance at the altar. For it is evident that our Lord hath sprung out of Judah ; as to which tribe Moses spake nothing concerning priests. And what we say is yet more abundantly evident, if after the likeness of Melchizedek there ariseth another Priest, Who hath been made, not after the law

of a carnal commandment, but after the power of an endless life : for
it is witnessed of Him,

> Thou art a Priest for ever
> After the order of Melchizedek.

For there is a disannulling of a foregoing commandment because of its
weakness and unprofitableness (for the Law made nothing perfect), and
a bringing in thereupon of a better hope, through which we draw nigh
unto God. And inasmuch as it is not without the taking of an oath
(for they indeed have been made priests without an oath; but He with
an oath by Him that saith of Him,

> The Lord sware and will not repent Himself,
> Thou art a Priest for ever) ;

by so much also hath Jesus become the Surety of a better covenant.
And they indeed have been made priests many in number, because that
by death they are hindered from continuing : but He, because He
abideth for ever, hath His priesthood unchangeable. Wherefore also
He is able to save to the uttermost them that draw near unto God
through Him, seeing He ever liveth to make intercession for them. For
such a High-priest became us, holy, guileless, undefiled, separated from
sinners, and made higher than the heavens ; Who needeth not daily, like
those high-priests, to offer up sacrifices, first for His own sins, and then
for the sins of the people : for this He did once for all, when He offered
up Himself. For the Law appointeth men high-priests, having infirmity; but the word of the oath, which was after the Law, appointeth
a Son, perfected for evermore."

CHAPTER VII.

THE ALLEGORY OF MELCHIZEDEK.

JESUS has entered heaven as our Forerunner, in virtue of His eternal priesthood. The endless duration and heavenly power of His priesthood is the "hard saying" which the Hebrew Christians would not easily receive, inasmuch as it involves the setting aside of the old covenant. But it rests on the words of the inspired Psalmist. Once already an inference has been drawn from the Psalmist's prophecy. The meaning of the Sabbath rest has not been exhausted in the Sabbath of Judaism; for David, so long after the time of Moses, speaks of another and better day. Similarly in the seventh chapter the Apostle finds an argument in the mysterious words of the Psalm, "The Lord hath sworn, and will not repent, Thou art a Priest for ever after the order of Melchizedek." *

The words are remarkable because they imply that in the heart of Judaism there lurked a yearning for

---

* Ps. cx. 1.

8

another and different kind of priesthood from that of Aaron's order. It may be compared to the strange intrusion now and again of other gods than the deities of Olympus into the religion of the Greeks, either by the introduction of a new deity or by way of return to a condition of things that existed before the young gods of the court of Zeus began to hold sway. But, to add to the mysterious character of the Psalm, it gives utterance to a desire for another King also, Who should be greater than a mere son of David: "The Lord said unto my Lord, Sit Thou at My right hand, until I make Thine enemies Thy footstool." Yet the Psalmist is David himself, and Christ silenced the Pharisees by asking them to explain the paradox: "If David then call Him Lord, how is He his Son?"* Delitzsch observes "that in no other psalm does David distinguish between himself and Messiah;" that is, in all his other predictions Messiah is David himself idealised, but in this Psalm He is David's Lord as well as his Son. The Psalmist desires a better priesthood and a better kingship.

These aspirations are alien to the nature of Judaism. The Mosaic dispensation pointed indeed to a coming priest, and the Jews might expect Messiah to be a King. But the Priest would be the antitype of Aaron,

---

* Matt. xxii. 45.

and the King would be only the Son of David. The Psalm speaks of a Priest after the order, not of Aaron, but of Melchizedek, and of a King Who would be David's Lord. To increase the difficulty, the Priest and the King would be one and the same Person.

Yet the Psalmist's mysterious conception comes to the surface now and again. In the Book of Zechariah the Lord commands the prophet to set crowns upon the head of Joshua the high-priest, and proclamation is made "that he shall be a priest upon his throne." * The Maccabæan princes are invested with priestly garments. Philo † has actually anticipated the Apostle in his reference to the union of the priesthood and kingship in the person of Melchizedek. We need not hesitate to say that the Apostle borrows his allegory from Philo, and finds his conception of the Priest-King in the religious insight of the profounder men, or at least in their earnest groping for better things. All this notwithstanding, his use of the allegory is original and most felicitous. He adds an idea fraught with consequences to his argument. For the central thought of the passage is the endless duration of the priesthood of Melchizedek. The Priest-King is Priest for ever.

We have spoken of Melchizedek's story as an alle-

---

* Zech. vi., 11 13.   † *SS. Legg. Alleg.*, iii. (vol. i., p. 103, Mang.).

gory, not to insinuate doubt of its historical truth, but because it cannot be intended by the Apostle to have direct inferential force. It is an instance of the allegorical interpretation of Old Testament events, similar to what we constantly find in Philo, and once at least in St. Paul. Allegorical use of history has just as much force as a parable drawn from nature, and comes just as near a demonstration as the types, if it is so used by an inspired prophet in the Scriptures of the Old Testament. This is precisely the difference between our author and Philo. The latter invents allegories and lets his fancy run wild in weaving new coincidences, which Scripture does not even suggest. But the writer of the Epistle to the Hebrews keeps strictly within the lines of the Psalm. We must also bear in mind that the story of Melchizedek sets forth a feature of Christ's priesthood which cannot be figured by a type of the ordinary form. Philo infers from the history of Melchizedek the sovereignty of God. The Psalmist and the Apostle teach from it the eternal duration of Christ's priesthood. But how can any type represent such a truth ? How can the fleeting shadow symbolise the notion of abiding substance ? The type by its very nature is transitory. That Christ is Priest for ever can be symbolically taught only by negations, by the absence of a beginning and of an end, in some such way as the hieroglyphics represent eternity by a line turning back upon itself. In this negative fashion, Melchizedek has been assimilated to the Son of God. His history was intentionally so related by God's Spirit that the sacred writer's silence even is significant. For Melchizedek suddenly appears on the scene, and as suddenly vanishes, never to return. Hitherto in the Bible story every man's descent is carefully noted, from the sons of Adam to Noah, from Noah down to Abraham. Now, however, for the first time, a man stands before us of whose genealogy and birth nothing is said. Even his death is not mentioned. What is known of him wonderfully helps the allegorical significance of the intentional silence of Scripture. He is king and priest, and the one act of his life is to bestow his priestly benediction on the heir of the promises. No more appropriate or more striking symbol of Christ's priesthood can be imagined.

His name even is symbolical. He is " King of righteousness." By a happy coincidence, the name of his city is no less expressive of the truth to be represented. He is King of Salem, which means " King of peace." The two notions of righteousness and peace combined make up the idea of priesthood. Righteousness without peace punishes the transgressor. Peace without righteousness condones the transgression. The kingship of Melchizedek, it appears, involves that he is priest.

This king-priest is a monotheist, though he is not of the family of Abraham. He is even priest of the Most High God, though he is outside the pale of the priesthood afterwards founded in the line of Aaron. Judaism, therefore, enjoys no monopoly of truth. As St. Paul argues that the promise is independent of the Law, because it was given four hundred years before, so our author hints at the existence of a priesthood distinct from the Levitical. What existed before Aaron may also survive him.

Further, these two men, Melchizedek and Abraham, were mutually drawn each to the other by the force of their common piety. Melchizedek went out to meet Abraham on his return from the slaughter of the kings, apparently not because he was indebted to him for his life and the safety of his city (for the kings had gone their way as far as Dan after pillaging the Cities of the Plain), but because he felt a strong impulse to bestow his blessing on the man of faith. He met him, not as king, but as priest. Would it be too fanciful to conjecture that Abraham had that mysterious power, which some men possess and some do not, of attracting to himself and becoming a centre, around which others almost unconsciously gather? It is suggested by his entire history. Whether it was so or not, Melchizedek blessed him, and Abraham accepted the blessing, and acknowledged its priestly character by giving him the priest's portion, the tenth of the best spoils. How great must this man have been, who blessed even Abraham, and to whom Abraham, the patriarch, paid even the tenth! But the less is blessed of the greater. In Abraham the Levitical priesthood itself may be said to acknowledge the superiority of Melchizedek.*

Wherein lay his greatness? He was not in the priestly line. Neither do we read that he was appointed of God. Yet no man taketh this honour unto himself. God had made him king and priest by conferring upon him the gift of innate spiritual greatness. He was one of nature's kings, born to rule, not because he was his father's son, but because he had a great soul. It is not in record that he bequeathed to his race a great idea. He created no school, and had no following. So seldom is mention made of him in the Old Testament, that the Psalmist's passing reference to his name attracts the Apostle's special notice. He became a priest in virtue of what he was as man. His authority as king sprang from character.

Such men appear on earth now and again. But they are never accounted for. All we can say of them is that they have neither father nor mother nor genealogy. They resemble those who are born of the Spirit, of whom we know neither whence they come nor

---

* Chap. vii. 6—10.

whither they go. It is only from the greatest one among these kings and priests of men that the veil is lifted. In Him we see the Son of God. In Christ we recognise the ideal greatness of sheer personality, and we at once say of all the others, as the Apostle says of Melchizedek, that they have been "made like," not unto ancestors or predecessors, but unto Him Who is Himself like His Divine Father.

Such priests remain priests for ever. They live on by the vitality of their priesthood. They have no beginning of days or end of life. They have never been set apart with outward ritual to an official distinction, marked by days and years. Their acts are not ceremonial, and wait not on the calendar. They bless men, and the blessing abides. They pray, and the prayer dies not. If their prayer lives for ever, can we suppose that they themselves pass away ? The king-priest is heir of immortality, whoever else may perish. He at least has the power of an endless life. If he dies in the flesh, he lives on in the spirit. An eternal heaven must be found or made for such men with God.

Now this is the gist and kernel of the Apostle's beautiful allegory. The argument points to the Son of God, and leads up to the conception of His eternal priesthood in the sanctuary of heaven. Let us see how the parable is interpreted and applied.

That Jesus is a great High-priest has been proved by

argument after argument from the beginning of the
Epistle. But this is not enough to show that the
priesthood after the order of Aaron has passed away.
The Hebrew Christians may still maintain that the
Messiah perfected the Aaronic priesthood and added to
it the glory of kingship. Transference of the priesthood must be proved; and it is symbolised in the
history of Melchizedek. But transference of the priesthood involves much more than what has hitherto been
mentioned. It implies, not merely that the priesthood
after the order of Aaron has come to an end, but that
the entire dispensation of law, the old covenant, is
replaced by a new covenant and a better one, inasmuch as the Law was erected on the foundation * of the
priesthood. It was a religious economy. The fundamental conceptions of the religion were guilt and
forgiveness. † The essential fact of the dispensation
was sacrifice offered for the sinner to God by a priest.
The priesthood was the article of a standing or a falling
Church under the Old Testament. Change of the
priesthood of itself abrogates the covenant.

What, then, is the truth in this matter ? Has the
priesthood been transferred ? Let the story of
Melchizedek, interpreted by the inspired Psalmist,
supply the answer.

---

* ἐπ' αὐτῆς (vii. 14).   † Cf. chap. vi. 1.

First, Jesus sprang from the royal tribe of Judah, not from the sacerdotal tribe of Levi. The Apostle intentionally uses a term * that glances at the prophet Zechariah's prediction concerning Him Who shall arise as the dawn, and be a Priest upon His throne. We shall, therefore, entitle Him " Lord," and say that " our *Lord*" has risen out of Judah.† He is Lord and King by right of birth. But this circumstance, that He belongs to the tribe of Judah, hints, to say the least, at a transference of the priesthood. For Moses said nothing of this tribe in reference to priests, however great it became in its kings. The kingship of our Lord is foreshadowed in Melchizedek.

Second, it is still more evident that the Aaronic priesthood has been set aside if we recall another feature in the allegory of Melchizedek. For Jesus is like Melchizedek as Priest, not as King only. The priesthood of Melchizedek sprang from the man's inherent greatness. How much more is it true of Jesus Christ that His greatness is personal ! He became what He is, not by force of law, which could create only an external, carnal commandment, but by innate power, in virtue of which He will live on and

---

* Ἀνατέταλκεν. Cf. Zech. vi. 12, Ἀνατολή, *dawn.* The citation, as usual, is from the Septuagint.
† Chap. vii. 14.

His life will be indestructible.* The commandment that constituted Aaron priest has not indeed been violently abrogated; but it has been thrust aside in consequence of its own inner feebleness and uselessness.† That it has been weak and unprofitable to men is evident from the inability of the Law, as a system erected upon that priesthood, to satisfy conscience.‡ Yet this carnal, decayed priesthood was permitted to linger on and work itself out. The better hope, through which we do actually come near unto God, did not forcibly put an end to it, but was superadded.§ Christ never formally abolished the old covenant. We cannot date its extinction. We must not say that it ceased to exist when the Supper was instituted, or when the true Passover was slain, or when the Spirit descended. The Epistle to the Hebrews is intended to awaken men to the fact that it is gone. They can hardly realise that it is dead. It has been lost, like the light of a star, in the spreading "dawn" of day. The sun of that eternal day is the infinitely great personality of Jesus Christ, born a crownless King; crowned at His death, but with thorns. Yet what mighty power He has wielded!

---

* Chap. vii. 16.
† ἀθέτησις, *a setting aside* (chap. vii. 18).
‡ οὐδὲν ἐτελείωσεν (vii. 19).
§ ἐπεισαγωγή.

The Galilæan has conquered. Since He has passed through the heavens from the eyes of men, thousands in every age have been ready to die for Him. Even to-day the Christianity of the greatest part of His followers consists more in profound loyalty to a personal King than in any intellectual comprehension of the Teacher's dogmatic system. Such kingly power cannot perish. Untouched by the downfall of king-doms and the revolutions of thought, such a King will sit upon His moral throne from age to age, yesterday and to-day the same, and for ever.

Third, the entire system or covenant based on the Aaronic priesthood has passed away and given place to a better covenant,—better in proportion to the firmer foundation on which the priesthood of Jesus rests.* Beyond question, the promises of God were steadfast. But men could not realise the glorious hope of their fulfilment, and that for two reasons. First, difficult conditions were imposed on fallible men. The worshipper might transgress in many points of ritual. His mediator, the priest, might err where error would be fatal to the result. Worshipper and priest, if they were thoughtful and pious men, would be haunted with the dread of having done wrong they knew not how or where, and be filled with dark forebodings. Confi-

---

* Chap. vii. 20--22.

dence, especially full assurance, was not to be thought
of. Second, Christ found it necessary to urge His
disciples to believe in God. The misery of distrusting
God Himself exists. Men think that He is such as
they are; and, as they do not believe in themselves,
their faith in God is a reed shaken by the wind. These
wants were not adequately met by the old covenant.
The conditions imposed perplexed men, and the revelation of God's moral character and Fatherhood was not
sufficiently clear to remove distrust. The Apostle
directs attention to the strange absence of any swearing
of an oath on the part of God when He instituted the
Aaronic priesthood, or on the part of the priest at his
consecration. Yet the kingship was confirmed by oath
to David. In the new covenant, on the other hand, all
such fears may be dismissed. For the only condition
imposed is faith. In order to make faith easy and
inspire men with courage, God appoints a Surety* for
Himself. He offers His Son as Hostage, and thus
guarantees the fulfilment of His promise. As the Man
Jesus, the Son of God was delivered into the hands of
men. "Of the better covenant Jesus is the Surety."
This will explain a word in the sixth chapter, which we
were compelled at the time to put aside. For it is
there said that God " mediated " with an oath.† We

---

* ἔγγυος.   † ἐμεσίτευσεν (vi. 17)

now understand that this means the appointment of
Christ to be Surety of the fulfilment of God's promises.
The old covenant could offer no guarantee. It is true
that it was ordained in the hands of a mediator. But
it is also true that the mediator was no surety, inasmuch as those priests were made without an oath.
Christ has been made Priest with an oath. Therefore
He is, as Jesus, the Surety of a better covenant. In
what respects the covenant is better, the Apostle will
soon tell us. For the present, we only know that the
foundation is stronger in proportion as the oath of
God reveals more fully His sincerity and love, and
renders it an easier thing for men laden with guilt to
trust the promise.

Before we dismiss the subject, it may be well to
remind the reader that this mention of a Surety by our
author is the *locus classicus* of the Federalist school of
divines. Cocceius and his followers present the whole
range of theological doctrines under the form of covenant. They explain the words "Surety of a better
covenant" to mean that Christ is appointed by God
to be a Surety on behalf of men, not on behalf of
God. The course of thought in the passage is, we
think, decisive against this interpretation. At the same
time, we readily admit that their doctrine is a just
theological inference from the passage. If God swears
that His gracious purposes will be fulfilled and ordains

Jesus to be His Surety to men, and if also the fulfilment of the Divine promise depends on the fulfilment of
certain conditions on the part of men, the oath of God
will involve His enabling men to fulfil those conditions,
and the Surety will become in eventual fact a Surety
on behalf of men. But this is only an inference. It
is not the meaning of the Apostle's words, who only
speaks of the Surety on the part of God. The validity
of the inference now mentioned depends on other considerations extraneous to this passage. With those
considerations, therefore, we have at present nothing
to do.

Fourth, the climax of the argument is reached when
the Apostle infers the endless duration of Christ's
one priesthood.* The number of men who had been
successively high-priests of the old covenant increased
from age to age. Dying one after another, they
were prevented from continuing as high-priests. But
Melchizedek had no successor; and the Jews themselves admitted that the Christ would abide for ever.
The ascending argument of the Apostle proves that He
ever liveth, and has, therefore, an immutable priesthood.
For, first, He is of the royal tribe, and the oath of God
to David guarantees that of his kingdom there shall be
no end. Again, in the greatness of His personality, He

---

* Chap. vii. 23—25.

is endowed with the power of an endless life. Moreover, as Priest He has been established in His office by oath. He is, therefore, Priest for ever.

A question suggests itself. Why is the endless life of one high-priest more effective than a succession, conceivably an endless succession, of high-priests? The eternal priesthood involves two distinct, but mutually dependent, conceptions,—power to save and intercession. In the case of any man, to live for ever means power. Even the body of our humiliation will be raised in power. Can the spirit, therefore, in the risen life, its own native home, be subject to weakness? What, then, shall we say of the risen and glorified Christ? The difference between Him and the high-priests of earth is like the difference between the body that is raised and the body that dies. In Aaron priesthood is sown in corruption, dishonour, weakness; in Christ priesthood is raised in incorruption, in glory, in power. In Aaron it is sown a natural priesthood; in Christ it is raised a spiritual priesthood. It must be that the High-priest in heaven has power to save continually and completely. Whenever help is needed, He is living. But He ever lives that He may intercede.* Apart from intercession on behalf of men, His power is not moral. It has no greatness, or joy, or meaning.

---

* Chap. vii. 25.

Intercession is the moral content of His powerful existence. Whenever help is needed, He is living, and is mighty * to save from sin, to rescue from death, to deliver from its fear.

To prove that Christ's eternal priesthood involves power and intercession is the purpose of the next verses.† Such a High-priest, powerful to save and ever living to intercede, is the only One befitting us, who are at once helpless and guilty. The Apostle triumphantly unfolds the glory of this conception of a high-priest. He means Christ. But he is too triumphant to name Him. "Such a high-priest befits us." The power of His heavenly life implies the highest development of moral condition. He will address God with holy reverence.‡ He will succour men without a tinge of malice, § which is but another way of saying that He wishes them well from the depth of His heart. He must not be sullied by a spot of moral defilement ‖ (for purity only can face God or love men). He must be set apart for His lofty function from the sinners for whom He intercedes. He must enter the true holiest place and stand in awful solitariness above the heavens of worlds and angels in the immediate presence of God. Further, He must not be under the necessity of leaving

---

* δύναται, the emphatic word in the passage.   † Chap. vii. 26.

‡ ὅσιος.   § ἄκακος.   ‖ ἀμίαντος.

the holiest place to renew His sacrifice, as the high-priests of the old covenant had need to offer, through the priests, new sacrifices every day through the year for themselves and for the people—yea, for themselves first, then for the people—before they dared re-enter within the veil.*   For Christ offered Himself.   Such a sacrifice, once offered, was sufficient for ever.

To sum up.†   The Law appoints men high-priests ; the word, which God has spoken unto us in His Son, appoints the Son Himself High-priest.   The Law appoints men high-priests in their weakness ; the word appoints the Son in His final and complete attainment of all perfection.   But the Law will yield to the word.   For the word, which had gone before the Law in the promise made to Abraham, was not super-seded by the Law, but came also after it in the stronger form of an oath, of which the old covenant knew nothing.

---

* Chap. vii. 27.   † Chap. vii. 28.

THE NEW COVENANT.

" Now in the things which we are saying the chief point *is this :* We have such a High-priest, Who sat down on the right hand of the throne of the Majesty in the heavens, a Minister of the sanctuary, and of the true tabernacle, which the Lord pitched, not man. For every high-priest is appointed to offer both gifts and sacrifices : wherefore it is necessary that this *High-priest* also have somewhat to offer. Now if He were on earth, He would not be a Priest at all, seeing there are those who offer the gifts according to the Law ; who serve *that which is* a copy and shadow of the heavenly things, even as Moses is warned *of God* when he is about to make the tabernacle : for, See, saith He, that thou make all things according to the pattern that was showed thee in the mount. But now hath He obtained a ministry the more excellent, by how much also He is the Mediator of a better covenant, which hath been enacted upon better promises."—HEB. viii. 1—6 (R.V.).

CHAPTER VIII.

THE NEW COVENANT.

THE Apostle has interpreted the beautiful story of Melchizedek with wonderful felicity and force. The point of the whole Epistle, he now tells us, lies there. He has brought forth the headstone of the corner, the keystone of the arch.* It is, in short, that we have such a High-priest. Country, holy city, ark of the covenant, all are lost. But if we have the High-priest, all are restored to us in a better and more enduring form. Jesus is the High-priest and King. He has taken His seat once for all, as King, on the right hand of the throne of the Majesty, and, as Priest, is also Minister of the sanctuary and of the true tabernacle. The indefinite and somewhat unusual term "minister" or "public servant" † is intentionally chosen, partly to emphasise the contrast between Christ's kingly dignity and His priestly service, partly because the author wishes to explain at greater length

---

* κεφάλαιον (viii. 1).   † λειτουργός (viii. 2).

in what Christ's actual work as High-priest in heaven
consists. For Christ's heavenly glory is a life of
service, not of selfish gratification. Every high-priest
serves.* He is appointed for no other purpose than
to offer gifts and sacrifices. The Apostle's readers
admitted that Christ was High-priest. But they were
forgetting that, as such, He too must necessarily
minister and have something which He can offer. Our
theology is still in like danger. We are sometimes
prone to regard Christ's life in heaven as only a state
of exaltation and power, and, consequently, to speak
more of the saints' happiness than of their service. It
is the natural result of superficial theories of the
Atonement that little practical use is made by many
Christians of the truth of Christ's priestly intercession.
The debt has been paid, the debtor discharged, and the
transaction ended. Christ's present activity towards
God is acknowledged and—neglected. Protestants are
confirmed in this baneful worldliness of conception by
their just desire to keep at a safe distance from the
error in the opposite extreme : that Christ presents to
God the Church's sacrifices of the mass.

The truth lies midway between two errors. On the
one hand, Christ's intercession is not itself the making
or constituting of a sacrifice; on the other, it is not

---

* Chap. viii. **3.**

mere pleading and prayer.   The sacrifice was made
and completed on the Cross, as the victims were slain
in the outer court.   But it was through the blood of
those victims the high-priest had authority to enter the
holiest place; and when he had entered, he must
sprinkle the warm blood, and so present the sacrifice
to God.   Similarly Christ must enter a sanctuary in
order to present the sacrifice slain on Calvary.   The
words of the Apostle John, " We have an Advocate with
the Father," express only one side of the truth.   But
he adds the other side of the conception in the same
verse, " And He is the propitiation," which is a very
different thing from saying, " His death was the
propitiation."   But what sanctuary shall He enter ?
He could not approach the holiest place in the earthly
temple.   For if He were on earth, He would not be
a Priest at all, seeing there are men ordained by the
Law to offer the appointed gifts on earth.*   The Jewish
priests have satisfied and exhausted the idea of an
earthly priesthood.   Even Melchizedek could not found
an order.   If he may be regarded as an attempt to
acclimatise on earth the priesthood of personal greatness,
the attempt was a failure.   It always fails, though it
is always renewed.   On earth there can be no order
of goodness.   When a great saint appears among men,

---

* Chap. viii. 4.

he is but a bird of passage, and is not to be found, because God has translated him.   If it is so of His saints, what of Christ ?   Christ on earth through the ages ?   Impossible !   And what is impossible to-day will be equally inconceivable at any point of time in the future.   A correct conception of Christ's priestly intercession is inconsistent with the dream of a reign of Christ on earth.   It may, or may not, be consistent with His kingly office.   But His priesthood forbids. We infer that Christ has transformed the heaven of glory into the holiest place of a temple, and the throne of God into a shrine before which He, as High-priest, presents His sacrifice.

The Jewish priesthood itself teaches the existence of a heavenly sanctuary.*   All the arrangements of tabernacle and ritual were made after a pattern shown to Moses on Mount Sinai.   The priests, in the tabernacle and through their ritual, ministered to the holiest place, as the visible image and outline of the real holiest place —that is, heaven—which the Lord pitched, not man.

Now Christ's more excellent ministry as High-priest in heaven carries in its bosom all that the Apostle contends for,—the establishment of a new covenant which has set aside for ever the covenant of the Law. "He has obtained a ministry the more excellent by

---

* Chap. viii. 5

how much He is the Mediator of a better covenant." *
These words contain in a nutshell the entire argument,
or series of arguments, that extends from the sixth
verse of the eighth chapter to the eighteenth verse of
the tenth. The course of thought may be divided as
follows : —

1. That the Lord intends to establish a new covenant is first of all shown by a citation from the prophet
Jeremiah (viii. 7— 13).

2. A description of the tabernacle and of the entrance of the priests and high-priests into it teaches
that the way into the holiest place was not yet open to
men. This is contrasted with the entering of Christ
into heaven through His own blood, which proves that
He has obtained for us an eternal redemption and is
Mediator of a new covenant, founded on His death
(ix. 1—18).

3. The frequent entering of the high-priest into the
holiest place is contrasted with the one death of Christ
and His entering heaven once. This proves the power
of His sacrifice and intercession to bring in the better
covenant and set aside the former one (ix. 25—x. 18).

I. A New Covenant promised through Jeremiah.

" For if that first covenant had been faultless, then would no place
have been sought for a second. For finding fault with them, He saith,

---

* Chap. viii. 6.

Behold, the days come, saith the Lord,
That I will make a new covenant with the house of Israel and
    with the house of Judah ;
Not according to the covenant that I made with their fathers
In the day that I took them by the hand to lead them forth out
    of the land of Egypt ;
For they continued not in My covenant,
And I regarded them not, saith the Lord.
For this is the covenant that I will make with the house of Israel
After those days, saith the Lord ;
I will put My laws into their mind,
And on their heart also will I write them :
And I will be to them a God,
And they shall be to Me a people :
And they shall not teach every man his fellow-citizen,
And every man his brother, saying, Know the Lord :
For all shall know Me,
From the least to the greatest of them.
For I will be merciful to their iniquities,
And their sins will I remember no more.

In that He saith, A new covenant, He hath made the first old. But
that which is becoming old and waxeth aged is nigh unto vanishing
away."—HEB. viii. 7—13 (R.V.).

The more spiritual men under the dispensation of
law anticipated a new and better era. The Psalmist
had spoken of another day, and prophesied of the
appearance of a Priest after the order of Melchizedek
and a Son of David Who would also be David's Lord.
But Jeremiah is very bold, and says * that the covenant
itself on which the hope of his nation hangs will pass
away, and his dream of a more spiritual covenant,

---

* Jer. xxxi. 31—34.

established on better promises, will at some distant day
come true. It is well to bear in mind that this discon-
tent with the present order lodged in the hearts, not of
the worst, but of the best and greatest, sons of Judaism.
It was the salt of their character, the life of their
inspiration, the message of their prophecy. In days of
national distress and despair, this star shone the
brighter for the darkness. The terrible shame of the
Captivity and the profound agony that followed it were
lit up with the glorious vision of a better future in store
for the people of God. On the quivering lips of the
prophet that " sat weeping," as he is described in the
Septuagint,* this strong hope found utterance. He
had washed the dust of worldliness from his eyes with
tears, and, therefore, saw more clearly than the men of
his time the threatened downfall of Judah and the
bright dawn beyond. In reading his prophecy of the
new covenant we almost cease to wonder that some
persons thought Jesus was Jeremiah risen from the
dead. The prophet's words have the same ring of
undaunted cheerfulness, of intense compassion, of
prophetic faith ; and Christ, as well as the Apostle,
cites His prediction that all shall be taught of God.†

Jeremiah blames the people.‡ But the Apostle infers

---

* Lamentations, *Preface.* † John vi. 45.
‡ αὐτούς (viii. 8).

that the covenant itself was not faultless, inasmuch as the prophet seeks, in his censure of the people, to make room for another covenant. We have already been told that there was on earth no room for the priesthood of Christ.* Similarly, in the sphere of earthly nationality, there was no room for a covenant other than that which God had made with His people Israel when He brought them out of the land of Egypt. But the earthly priesthood could not give efficacy to its ministering, and thus room is found for a heavenly priesthood. So also, the covenant on which the earthly priesthood rested being inadequate, the prophet makes room for the introduction of a new and better covenant.

Now the peculiar character of the old covenant was that it dealt with men in the aggregate which we call the nation. Nationalism is the distinctive feature of the old world, within the precincts of Judaism and among the peoples of heathendom. Even the prophets could not see the spiritual truth, which they themselves foretold, except through the medium of nationality. The Messiah was the national king idealised, even when He was a Man of sorrows and acquainted with grief. In the passage before us the prophet Jeremiah speaks of God's promise to write His law on the heart as made to the house of Judah and the house of Israel, as if he

---

* Chap. viii. 4.

were not aware that, in so speaking, he was really con-
tradicting himself. For the blessing promised was a
spiritual and, consequently, personal one, with which
nationality cannot possibly have any sort of connection.
It is a matter of profound joy to every lover of his
people to witness and share in the uprising of a national
consciousness. Some among us are beginning to know
now for the first time that a national ideal is possible
in thought, and sentiment, and life. But there must not,
cannot, be a nationality in religion. A moral law in
the heart does not recognise the quality of the blood
that circulates through. This truth the prophets strove
to utter, often in vain. Yet the breaking up of the
nation into Judah and Israel helped to dispel the
illusion. The loss of national independence prepared
for the universalism of Jesus Christ and St. Paul.
Now also, when an epistle is written to the Hebrew
Christians, the threatened extinction of nationality
drives men to seek the bond of union in a more stable
covenant, which will save them, if anything can, from
the utter collapse of all religious fellowship and civil
society. It is the glory of Christianity that it creates
the individual and at the same moment keeps perfectly
clear of individualism. Its blessings are personal, but
they imply a covenant. If nationalism has been
dethroned, individualism has not climbed to the
vacant seat. How it achieves this great result will

be understood from an examination of Jeremiah's prophecy.

The new covenant deals with the same fundamental conceptions which dominated the former one. These are the moral law, knowledge of God, and forgiveness of sin. So far the two dispensations are one. Because these great conceptions lie at the root of all human goodness, religion is essentially the same thing under both covenants. There is a sense in which St. Augustine was right in speaking of the saints under the old Testament as "Christians before Christ." Judaism and Christianity stand shoulder to shoulder over against the religious ideas and practices of all the heathen nations of the world. But in Judaism these sublime conceptions are undeveloped. Nationalism dwarfs their growth. They are like seeds falling on the thorns, and the thorns grow up and choke them. God, therefore, spoke unto the Jews in parables, in types and shadows. Seeing, they saw not; and hearing, they heard not, neither did they understand.

Because the former covenant was a national one, the conceptions of the moral law, of God, of sin and its forgiveness, would be narrow and external. The moral law would be embedded in the national code. God would be revealed in the history of the nation. Sin would consist either in faults of ignorance and inadvertence or in national apostasy from the theocratic

King. In these three respects the new covenant excels,
—in respect, that is, of the moral law, knowledge of
God, and forgiveness of sin, which yet may be justly
regarded as the three sides of the revelation given
under the former covenant.

1. The moral law will either forget its own holiness,
righteousness, and goodness, and degenerate into
national rules of conduct, or else, by the innate force
of its spirituality, create in men a consciousness of sin
and a strong desire for reconciliation with God. Men
will resist, and, when resistance is vain, will chafe
against its terrible strength. "The Law came in
beside, that the trespass might abound." * But it often
happens that guilt of conscience is the alarum that
awakens moral self-consciousness out of sleep, never to
fall asleep again when holiness has found entrance into
the soul. Beyond this the old covenant advanced not a
step. The promise of the new covenant is to put the
Law into the mind, not in an ark of shittim wood, and
to write it in the heart, not on tables of stone. The
Law was given on Sinai as an external commandment;
it is put into the mind as a knowledge of moral truth.
It was written on the two tables in the weakness of the
letter; on the heart it is written as a principle and a
power of obedience. The power of God to command

* Rom. v. 20.

becomes the strength of man to obey. In this way the new covenant realises what the former covenant demanded. The new covenant is the old covenant transformed, made spiritual. God is become the God of His people; and this was the promise of the former covenant. They are no more children, as they were when God took them by the hand and led them out of the land of Egypt. Instead of the external guidance, they have the unction within, and know all things. Renewed in the spirit of their mind, they put on the new man, which after God is created in righteousness and the holiness of truth.

2. So also of knowing God. The moral attributes of the Most High are revealed under the former covenant, and the God of the Old Testament is the God of the New. Abraham knows Him as the everlasting God. Elisha understands that there is no darkness or shadow of death where the workers of iniquity may hide themselves. Balaam declares that God is not a man that He should lie. The Psalmist confesses to God that he cannot flee from His presence. The father of believers fears not to ask, " Shall not the Judge of the earth do right?" Moses recognises that the Lord is longsuffering, and of great mercy, forgiving iniquity and transgression. Isaiah hears the seraphim crying one to another, " Holy, holy, holy, is the Lord of hosts." But nationalism distorted the image. The

conception of God's Fatherhood is most indistinct. When, however, Christ taught His disciples to say in prayer, " Our Father," He could then at once add the words " Who art in heaven." The spirit of man rose immediately with a mighty upheaval above the narrow bounds of nationalism. The attributes of God became more lofty as well as more amiable to the eyes of His children. The God of a nation is not great enough to be our Father. The God Who is our Father is God in heaven.

Not only are God's attributes revealed, but the faculty to know Him is also bestowed. The moral law and a heart to love it are the two elements of a knowledge of God's nature. For God Himself is holiness and love. In vain will men cry one to another, saying, " Know the Lord." As well might they bid the blind behold the light, or the wicked love purity. Knowledge of nature can be taught. It can be parcelled in propositions, carried about, and handed to others. But the character of God is not a notion, and cannot be taught as a lesson or in a creed, however true the creed may be. The two opposite ends of all our knowledge are our sensations and God. In one respect the two are alike. Knowledge of them cannot be conveyed in words.

3. The only thing concerning God that can be known by a man who is not holy himself is that He will punish

the impenitent, and can forgive. These are objective facts.
They may be announced to the world, and believed. In
the history of all holy men, under the Old Testament
as well as under the New, they are their first lesson
in spiritual theology. To say that penitent sinners
under the Law could not be absolved from guilt or taste
the sweetness of God's forgiving grace must be false.
St. Paul himself, who describes the Law as a covenant
that "gendereth to bondage," cites the words of the
Psalmist, "Blessed is he whose transgression is forgiven, whose sin is covered," to prove that God imputes
righteousness without works.* When the Apostle
Peter was declaring that all the prophets witness to
Jesus Christ, that through His name whosoever be-
lieveth in Him shall receive remission of sins, the Holy
Ghost fell on all who heard the word. The very
promise which Jeremiah says will be fulfilled under the
future covenant Isaiah claims for his own days: "I,
even I, am He that blotteth out thy transgressions for
Mine own sake, and will not remember thy sins." †

On the other hand, it is equally plain that St. Paul
and the author of this Epistle agree in teaching that
the sacrifices of the old covenant had in them no
virtue to remove guilt. They cannot take away sin,
and they cannot remove the consciousness of sin.‡ The

---

* Rom. iv. 7.   † Isa. xliii. 25.   ‡ Chap. x. 2, 4.

writer evidently considers it sufficient to state the impossibility, without labouring to prove it. His readers' consciences would bear him out in the assertion that it is not possible that the blood of bulls and of goats should take away sins.

It remains—and it is the only supposition left to us—that peace of conscience must have been the result of another revelation, simultaneous with the covenant of the Law, but differing from it in purpose and instruments. Such a revelation would be given through the prophets, who stood apart as a distinct order from the priesthood. They were the preachers. They quickened conscience, and spoke of God's hatred of sin and willingness to forgive. Every advance in the revelation came through the prophets, not through the priests. The latter represent the stationary side of the covenant, but the prophets hold before the eyes of men the idea of progress. What, then, was the weakness of prophecy in reference to forgiveness of sin when compared with the new covenant? The prophets predicted a future redemption. This was their strength. It was also their weakness. For that future was not balanced by an equally great past. However glorious the history of the nation had been, it was not strong enough to bear the weight of so transcendent a future. Every nation that believes in the greatness of its own future already possesses a great past. If not, it creates one. Mythology and hero-worship are the attempt of a people to erect their future on a sufficient foundation. But men had not experienced anything great enough to inspire them with a living faith in the reality of the promises which the prophets announced. Sin had not been atoned for. The Christian preacher can point to the wonderful but well-assured facts of the life and death of Jesus Christ. If he could not do this, or if he neglects to do it, feeble and unreal will sound his proclamation of the terrors and joys of the world to come. The Gospel has for one of its primary objects to appease the guilty conscience. How it achieves this purpose our author will tell us in another chapter. For the present all we learn is that knowledge of God is knowledge of His moral nature, and that this knowledge belongs to the man whose moral consciousness has been quickened. The evangelical doctrine that the source of holiness is thankfulness was well meant, as an antidote to legalism on the one hand and to Antinomianism on the other. The sinner, we were told, once redeemed from the curse of the Law and delivered from the danger of perdition, begins to love the Christ Who redeemed and saved him. The doctrine contains a truth, and is applicable to this extent; that he to whom much is forgiven loveth much. But it would not be true to say that all good men have sought God's forgiveness because they feared hell torments. To some their guilt is their hell. Fear is too narrow a foundation of holiness. We cannot explain saintliness by mere gratitude. For "thankfulness" we must write "conscience," and substitute forgiveness and absolution from guilt for safety from future misery, if we would lay a foundation broad and firm enough on which to erect the sublimest holiness of man.

Our author infers from the words of Jeremiah that there was an inherent decay in the former covenant. It was itself ready to vanish away, and make room for a new and more spiritual one.[*]

II. A New Covenant symbolized in the Tabernacle.

" Now even the first covenant had ordinances of divine service, and its sanctuary, a sanctuary of this world. For there was a tabernacle prepared, the first, wherein were the candlestick, and the table, and the shewbread ; which is called the Holy place. And after the second veil, the tabernacle which is called the Holy of holies ; having a golden censer, and the ark of the covenant overlaid round about with gold, wherein was a golden pot holding the manna, and Aaron's rod that budded, and the tables of the covenant ; and above it cherubim of glory overshadowing the mercy-seat ; of which we cannot now speak severally. Now these things having been thus prepared, the priests go in continually into the first tabernacle, accomplishing the services ; but into the second the high-priest alone, once in the year, not without blood, which he offereth for himself, and for the errors of the people : the Holy Ghost this signifying, that the way into the holy place hath not yet been made manifest, while as the first tabernacle is yet standing ; which is a parable for the time now present ; according to which are

* Chap. viii. 13.

offered both gifts and sacrifices that cannot, as touching the conscience, make the worshipper perfect, being only (with meats and drinks and divers washings) carnal ordinances, imposed until a time of reformation. But Christ having come a High-priest of the good things to come, through the greater and more perfect tabernacle, not made with hands, that is to say, not of this creation, nor yet through the blood of goats and calves, but through His own blood, entered in once for all into the holy place, having obtained eternal redemption. For if the blood of goats and bulls, and the ashes of a heifer sprinkling them that have been defiled, sanctify unto the cleanness of the flesh : how much more shall the blood of Christ, Who through the eternal Spirit offered Himself without blemish unto God, cleanse your conscience from dead works to serve the living God?"—HEB. ix. 1—14 (R.V.).

With the words of a prophet the Apostle contrasts the ritual of the priests. Jeremiah prophesied of a better covenant, because he found the former one did not satisfy conscience. A description of the tabernacle, its furniture and ordinances of Divine service, follows. At first it appears strange that the author should have thought it necessary to enumerate in detail what the tabernacle contained. But to infer that he is a Hellenist, to whom the matter had all the charm of novelty, would be very precarious. His purpose is to show that the way of the holiest was not yet open. The tabernacle consisted of two chambers : the foremost and larger of the two, called the sanctuary, and an inner one, called the holiest of all. Now the sanctuary had its furniture and stated rites. It was not a mere vestibule or passage leading to the holiest. The eighth verse, literally rendered, expresses that the outer sanc-

tuary "held a position."* Its furniture was for daily use.
The candelabrum supported the seven lamps, which
gave light to the ministering priests. The shewbread,
laid on the table in rows of twelve cakes, was eaten by
Aaron and his sons. Into this chamber the priests
went always, accomplishing the daily services. Moreover, between the holy place and the holiest of all
hung a thick veil. Into the holiest the high-priest
only was permitted to enter, and he could only enter
on the annual day of atonement. This chamber also
had its proper furniture. To it belonged † the altar of
incense (for so we must read in the fourth verse,
instead of "golden censer"), although its actual place
was in the outer sanctuary. It stood in front of
the veil that the high-priest might take the incense
from it, without which he was not permitted to enter
the holiest; and when he came out, he sprinkled it
with blood as he had sprinkled the holiest place itself.
In the inner chamber stood the ark of the covenant,
containing the pot of manna, Aaron's rod that budded,
and the two tables of stone on which the Ten Commandments were written. On the ark was the mercy-
seat, and above the mercy-seat were the cherubim.
But there were no lamps to give light; there was no
shewbread for food. The glory of the Lord filled it,

---

* ἐχούσης στάσιν (ix. 8).   † ἔχουσα (ix. 4).

and was the light thereof.   When the high-priest had
performed the atoning rites, he was not permitted to
stay within.   It is evident that reconciliation through
blood was the idea symbolized by the holiest place, its
furniture, and the yearly rite performed within it.   But
the veil and the outer chamber stood between the sinful
people and the mercy-seat.   Our author ascribes this
arrangement of the two chambers, the veil, and the one
entrance every year of the high-priest into the inner
shrine, to the Holy Spirit, Who teaches men by symbol*
that the way to God is not yet open.   But He also
teaches them through the ordinances of the outer
sanctuary that access to God is a necessity of conscience, and yet that the gifts and sacrifices there
offered cannot satisfy conscience, resting, as they
do, only on meats and drinks and divers washings.
All we can say of them is that they were the requirements of natural conscience, here termed "flesh," and
that these demands of human consciousness of guilt
were sanctioned and imposed on men by God provi-
sionally, until the time came for restoring permanently
the long-lost peace between God and men.

Contrast with all this the ministry of Christ.   He
made His appearance on earth as High-priest of the
things which have now at length come to us.†   The

---

* δηλοῦντος (ix. 8).   † Reading γενομένων (ix. 11).

blessings prophesied by Jeremiah have been realised. As High-priest He entered the true holiest place, a tabernacle greater and more perfect, even heaven itself.* It is greater; that is, larger.   The outer sanctuary has ceased to exist, because the veil has been rent in twain, and the holy place has been taken into the holiest place.   The tabernacle has now only one chamber, and in that chamber God meets all His worshipping saints, who come to Him through and with Jesus, the High-priest.   The tabernacle of God is with men, and He shall dwell, as in the tabernacle, with them, and they shall be His peoples, and God Himself shall be with them.†   Yea, the holiest place has spread itself over Mount Zion, on which stood the king's palace, and over the whole city of Jerusalem, which lieth four-square, and is become the heavenly and holy city, having no temple, because the Lord God Almighty and the Lamb are the temple thereof.   " And the city hath no need of the sun, neither of the moon, to shine upon it ; for the glory of God lightens it, and the lamp thereof is the Lamb."   The city and the holiest place are commensurate.   So large, indeed, is the holiest that the nations shall walk amidst the light thereof.   It is also more perfect.‡   For Christ has entered into the pre-

---

* Chap. ix. 11.   Cf. chap. ix. 24.

† Rev. xxi. 3.

‡ τελειοτέρας (ix. 11).

sence of God for us. Such a tabernacle is not constructed of the materials of this world,* nor fashioned
with the hands of cunning artificers, Bezaleel and
Aholiab. When Christ destroyed the sanctuary made
with hands, in three days He built another made
without hands. In a true sense it is not made at all,
not even by the hands of Him Who built all things;
for it is essentially God's presence. Into this holiest
place Christ entered, to appear in the immediate presence of God. But the Apostle is not satisfied with
saying that He entered within. Ten thousand times
ten thousand of His saints will do this. He has done
more. He went *through* † the holiest. He has passed
through the heavens.‡   He has been made higher than
the heavens.§   He has taken His seat on the right
hand of God. ‖   The Melchizedek Priest has ascended
to the mercy-seat and made it His throne. He is
Himself henceforth the shechinah, and the manifested
glory of the unseen Father. All this is expressed in
the words "through a greater and more perfect tabernacle."

Moreover, the high-priest entered into the holiest
place in virtue of the blood of goats and calves.¶   Add,
if you will, the ceremony of cleansing a person who had

---

* κοσμικόν (ix. 2).   ‡ Chap. iv. 14.   ‖ Chap. x. 12.
† διά (ix. 11).   § Chap. vii. 26.   ¶ Chap. ix. 12.

contracted defilement by touching a dead body.*   He
also was cleansed by having the ashes of a heifer
sprinkled upon his flesh.   Why, the very defilement is
unreal and artificial.   To touch a dead body a sin !   It
may have been well to make it a crime from sanitary
considerations, and it may become a sin because God
has forbidden it.   So far it touched conscience.   When
Elijah stretched himself upon the dead child of the
widow of Zarephath three times, and the soul of the
child came into him again, or when Elisha put his
mouth upon the mouth of the dead son of the Shunam-
mite, his eyes upon his eyes, and his hands upon his
hands, and the flesh of the child waxed warm, God's
holy prophet was defiled !   The mother and the child
might bring their thank-offering to the sanctuary ; but
the prophet, who had done the deed of power and
mercy, was excluded from joining in thanksgiving and
prayer.   If the defilement is unreal, what shall we
think of the means of cleansing ?   To touch a dead
child defiles, but the touch of the ashes of a burnt
heifer cleanses !   Yet natural conscience felt guilty
when thus defiled, and recovered itself, in some
measure, from its shame when thus made clean.†
Such men resemble the persons, referred to by St. Paul,
who have " a conscience of the idol." ‡   Judaism en-

---

* Chap. ix. 13.   † ἀγιάζει (ix. 13).   ‡ 1 Cor. viii. 7.

feebled the conscience. A man of morbid religious sentiment is often defiled in his own eyes by what is not really wrong, and often finds peace and comfort in what is not really a propitiation or a forgiveness.

On the other hand, Christ entered the true holiest place by His own blood. He offered Himself. The High-priest is the sacrifice. Under the old covenant the victim must be " without spot." But the high-priest was not without blemish, and he offered for himself as well as for the errors of the people. But in the offering of Christ, the spotless purity of the Victim ensures that the High-priest Himself is holy, harmless, undefiled, separate from sinners. For this reason it is said here* that He offered Himself "through an eternal spirit," or, as we should say in modern phrase, "through His eternal personality." He is the High-priest after the order of Melchizedek ; and He invests the sacrifice with all the personal greatness of the High-priest. Is He "without beginning of days or end of life"? So also His sacrifice abides for ever. His power of an indissoluble life belongs to His atonement. Is He untouched by the rolling stream of time ? His death was of infinite merit in reference to the past and to the future, though it took place historically at the end of the ages. His eternal personality made it

---

* Chap. ix. 14.

unnecessary for Him to suffer often since the foundation of the world. Because of His personal greatness, it sufficed that He should suffer once only and enter once into the holiest place. The eternal High-priest in one transitory act of death offered a sacrifice that remains eternally, and obtains for us an eternal redemption. If, then, the blood of goats and bulls and the ashes of an heifer appease, in some measure, the weak, frightened conscience of unenlightened nature, how much more shall the conscious, voluntary sacrifice of this eternal, personal Son deliver the conscience of him who worships, not a phantom deity, but an eternal, personal, living God, from the guilt of dead works, and bring him to worship that living God with an eternal, living personality!

Mark the contrasted notions. The brute life, dragged to the altar, little knowing that its hot blood is to be a propitiation for human guilt, is contrasted with the blood of the Christ (for there is but one), Who, with the consciousness and strength of an eternal personality, willingly offers Himself as a sacrifice. Between these two lives are all the lives which God created, human and angelic. Yet the offering of a beast in some fashion and to some degree appeased conscience, unillumined by the fierce light of God's holiness and untouched by the pathos of Christ's death. With this imperfect and negative peace, or, to speak more correctly, truce, of

conscience is contrasted the living, eager worship of
him whose enlightened conscience has been purified
from spiritual defilement by the blood of Christ.   Such
a man's entire service is worship, and his worship is
the ministering of a priest.*   He stands in the congregation of the righteous, and ascends unto God's holy
hill.   He enters the holiest place with Christ.   He
draws near with boldness to the mercy-seat, now the
very throne itself of grace.

It will be seen, if we have rightly traced the line
of thought, that the outer sanctuary no longer exists.
The larger and more perfect tabernacle is the holiest
place itself, when the veil has been removed, and the
sanctuary and courts are all included in the expanded
holiest.   Several very able expositors deny this.   They
find an antitype of the holy place either in the body of
Christ or in the created heavens, through which He has
passed into the immediate presence of God.   But this
introduces confusion, adds nothing of value to the
meaning of the type, and is inconsistent with our
author's express statement that the way into the
holiest was not yet open so long as the holy place stood.

III. A New Covenant ratified in the Death of Christ.

" And for this cause He is the Mediator of a new covenant, that a death
having taken place for the redemption of the transgressions that were

---

* λατρεύειν (ix. 14).

under the first covenant, they that have been called may receive the promise of the eternal inheritance. For where a testament is, there must of necessity be the death of him that made it. For a testament is of force where there hath been death ; for doth it ever avail while he that made it liveth ? Wherefore even the first covenant hath not been dedicated without blood. For when every commandment had been spoken by Moses unto all the people according to the Law, he took the blood of the calves and the goats, with water and scarlet wool and hyssop, and sprinkled both the book itself, and all the people, saying, This is the blood of the covenant which God commanded to you-ward. Moreover the tabernacle and all the vessels of the ministry he sprinkled in like manner with the blood. And according to the Law, I may almost say, all things are cleansed with blood, and apart from shedding of blood there is no remission. It was necessary therefore that the copies of the things in the heavens should be cleansed with these ; but the heavenly things themselves with better sacrifices than these. For Christ entered not into a holy place made with hands, like in pattern to the true ; but into heaven itself, now to appear before the face of God for us : nor yet that He should offer Himself often ; as the high-priest entereth into the holy place year by year with blood not his own ; else must He often have suffered since the foundation of the world : but now once at the end of the ages hath He been manifested to put away sin by the sacrifice of Himself. And inasmuch as it is appointed unto men once to die, and after this cometh judgment ; so Christ also, having been once offered to bear the sins of many, shall appear a second time, apart from sin, to them that wait for Him, unto salvation. For the Law having a shadow of the good *things* to come, not the very image of the things, they can never with the same sacrifices year by year, which they offer continually, make perfect them that draw nigh. Else would they not have ceased to be offered, because the worshippers, having been once cleansed, would have had no more con-science of sins ? But in those *sacrifices* there is a remembrance made of sins year by year. For it is impossible that the blood of bulls and goats should take away sins. Wherefore when He cometh into the world, He saith,

> Sacrifice and offering Thou wouldest not,
> But a body didst Thou prepare for Me ;

> In whole burnt offerings and *sacrifices* for sin Thou hadst no
>   pleasure :
> Then said I, Lo, I am come
> (In the roll of the book it is written of Me)
> To do Thy will, O God.

Saying above, Sacrifices and offerings and whole burnt offerings and
sacrifices for sin Thou wouldest not, neither hadst pleasure therein (the
which are offered according to the Law), then hath He said, Lo, I am
come to do Thy will.   He taketh away the first, that He may establish
the second.   By which will we have been sanctified through the offering
of the body of Jesus Christ once for all.   And every priest indeed
standeth day by day ministering and offering oftentimes the same
sacrifices, the which can never take away sins : but He, when He had
offered one sacrifice for sins for ever, sat down on the right hand of
God ; from henceforth expecting till His enemies be made the footstool
of His feet.   For by one offering He hath perfected for ever them that
are sanctified.   And the Holy Ghost also beareth witness to us : for
after He hath said,

> This is the covenant that I will make with them
> After those days, saith the Lord ;
> I will put My laws on their heart,
> And upon their mind also will I write them ;

then saith He,
    And their sins and their iniquities will I remember no more.
Now where remission of these is, there is no more offering for sin."—
HEB. ix. 15—x. 18 (R.V.).

The Apostle has proved that a new covenant was
promised through the prophet and prefigured in
the tabernacle.   Christ is come to earth and entered
into the holiest place of God, as High-priest.   The
inference is that His high-priesthood has abolished the
old covenant and ratified the new.   The priesthood
has been changed, and change of the priesthood implies

change of the covenant.   In fact, to this priesthood
the rites of the former covenant pointed, and on it the
priestly absolution rested.   Sins were forgiven, but not
in virtue of any efficacy supposed to belong to the rites
or sacrifices, all of which were types of another and
infinitely greater death.   For a death has taken place
for the redemption of all past transgressions, which
had been accumulating under the former covenant.
Now at length sin has been put out of the way.   The
heirs of the promise made to Abraham, centuries before
the giving of the Law, come at last into possession of
their inheritance.   The call has sounded.   The hour
has struck.   For this inheritance they waited till Christ
should die.   The earthly Canaan may pass from one
race to another race; but the unchangeable, eternal *
inheritance, into which none but the rightful heirs can
enter, is incorruptible, undefiled, fading not away,
reserved in heaven for those who are kept † for its
possession.

Because possession of it was delayed till Christ died,
it may be likened to an inheritance bequeathed by a
testator in his last will.   For when a person leaves
property by will to another, the will is of no force, the
transference is not actually made, the property does
not change hands, in the testator's lifetime.   The

---

* αἰωνίου (ix. 15).

† τετηρημένην . . . φρουρουμένους (1 Pet. i. 4).

transaction takes place after and in consequence of his death. This may serve as an illustration. Its pertinence as such is increased by the fact, which in all probability suggested it to our author, that the same word would be used by a Hebrew, writing in Greek, for " covenant," and by a native of Greece for " a testamentary disposition of property." * But it is only an illustration. We cannot suppose that it was intended to be anything more.†

To return to argument, the blood of Christ may be shown to have ratified a covenant from the use of blood by Moses to inaugurate the former covenant. The Apostle has spoken before of the shedding and sprinkling of blood in sacrifice. When the high-priest entered into the holiest place, he offered blood for himself and the people. But, besides its use in sacrifice, blood was sprinkled on the book of the law, on the tabernacle, and on all the vessels of the ministry. Without a copious stream, a veritable " outflow " ‡ of blood, both as ratifying the covenant and as offered in sacrifice,

---

* διαθήκη.

† To forestall censure for inconsistency, the present writer may be permitted to refer to what he now sees to have been a desperate attempt on his part (in the *Expositor*) to explain the passage on the supposition that the word διαθήκη means " covenant " throughout. He is bound to admit that the attempt was a failure. If he lives to write retractations, this will be one.

‡ αἱματεκχυσίας (ix. 22).

there was under the Law no remission of sins. Now
the typical character of all the arrangements and
ordinances instituted by Moses is assumed throughout.
Even the purification of the tabernacle and its vessels
with blood must be symbolical of a spiritual truth.
There is, therefore, in the new covenant a purification
of the true holiest place. To make the matter still
more evident, the author reminds his readers of a fact,
which he has already mentioned,* in reference to the
construction of the tabernacle. Moses was admonished
of God to make it a copy and shadow of heavenly
things. "For, See, saith He, that thou make all things
according to the pattern showed to thee in the mount."
It appears, then, that not only the covenant was
typical, but the tabernacle, its vessels, and the purify-
ing of all with blood were a copy of things in the
heavens, the true holiest place. And, inasmuch as the
holiest place has now, in Christ, included within it the
sanctuary, and every veil and wall of partition has
been removed, the purification of the tabernacle corresponds to a purification, under the new covenant, of
heaven itself.

Not that the heaven of God is polluted. Even the
earthly shrine had not itself contracted defilement.
The blood sprinkled on the tabernacle and its vessels

---

* Chap. viii. 5.

was not different from the blood of the sacrifice. As
sacrificial blood, it consecrated the place, and was also
offered to God. Similarly the blood of Christ made
heaven a sanctuary, erected there a holiest place for
the appearing of the great High-priest, constituted the
throne of the Most High a mercy-seat for men. By
the same act it became an offering to God, enthroned
on the mercy-seat. The two notions of ratifying the
covenant and atoning for sin cannot be separated. For
this reason our author says the heavenly things are
purified with *sacrifices.* But as heaven is higher than
the earth, as the true holiest place excels the typical,
so must the sacrifices that purify heaven be better than
the sacrifices that purified the tabernacle. But Christ
is great enough to make heaven itself a new place,
whereas He Himself remains unchanged, "yesterday
and to-day the same, and for ever."

The thought of Christ's eternal oneness is apparently
suggested to the Apostle by the contrast between Christ
and the purified heaven. But it helps his argument.
For the blood of Christ, when offered in heaven, so
fully and perfectly ratified the new covenant that He
remains for evermore in the holiest place and evermore
offers Himself to God in one eternally unbroken act.
He did not enter heaven to come out again, as the high-
priests presented their offering repeatedly, year after
year. They could not do otherwise, because they

entered "with blood not their own," or, as we may
render the word, "with alien * blood." The blood of
goats and bulls cannot take away sin. Consequently,
the absolution obtained is unreal and, therefore,
temporary in its effect. The blood of the beasts must
be renewed as the annual day of atonement comes
round. If Christ's offering of Himself had only a
temporary efficacy, He must often have suffered since
the foundation of the world. The forgiveness under
the former covenant put off the retribution for one
year. St. Paul expresses the same conception when
he describes it as not a real forgiveness, but as "the
passing over † of the sins done aforetime, in the for-
bearance of God." The writer of the Epistle infers that,
if Christ's sacrifice were meritorious for a time only,
then He ought to have repeated His offering whenever
the period for which it was efficacious came to an end;
and, inasmuch as His atonement was not restricted to
one nation, it would have been necessary for Him to
appear on earth repeatedly, and repeatedly die, not
from the time of Moses or of Abraham, but from the
foundation of the world. But our author has long
since said "that the works were finished from the
foundation of the world." ‡ God Himself after the

---

* ἀλλοτρίῳ (ix. 25).

† πάρεσιν, as contrasted with ἄφεσις (Rom. iii. 25).

‡ Chap. iv. 3.

work of creation entered on His Sabbath rest. The
Sabbath developed from initial creation to final atonement, and, because Christ's atonement is final, He has
perfected the Sabbath eternally in the heavens. But
the Sabbath of God would have been no Sabbath to
the Son of God, but a constant recurrence of sufferings
and deaths, if He did not finish transgression and
atone for sin by His one death. " Once, at the end
of the ages," when the tale of sin and woe has been
all told, " hath He appeared," which proves that He has
finally and for ever put away sin through His one
sacrifice.*

The Apostle speaks as one who believed that the end
of the world was at hand. He even builds an argument on this to him assured fact of the near future.
True, the end of the world was not yet. But the
argument is equally valid in its essential bearing. For
the important point is that Christ appeared on earth
only once. Whether His one death occurred at the
beginning of human history, or at the end, or at the
end of one period and the beginning of another, is
immaterial.

Then follows a very original piece of reasoning,
plainly intended to be an additional proof that Christ's
dying once put away sin for ever. To appear on earth

---

often, and to die often, would have been impossible for
Him.   He was true man, of woman born, not an
apparition, not an angel assuming the appearance of
humanity, not the Son of God really and man only
seemingly.   But it is appointed unto men once, and
only once, to die.   After their one death comes, sooner
or later, judgment.   To return to earth and make a new
beginning, to retrieve the errors and failures of a completed life, is not given to men.   This is the Divine
appointment.   Exception to the Apostle's argument
must not be taken from the resurrection of Lazarus and
others who were restored to life.   The Apostle speaks
of God's usual course of action.   So understood, it is
difficult to conceive how any words can be more
decisive against the doctrine of probation after death.
For, however long judgment may tarry, our author
acknowledges no possibility of changing any man's
state or character between death and the final award.
On this impossibility of retrieving the past the force of
the argument entirely depends.   If Christ, Who was
true man, failed in His one life and one death, the
failure is irretrievable.   He cannot come again to earth
and try anew.   To Him, as to other men, it was
appointed to die once only.   In His case, as in the
case of others, judgment follows death,—judgment
irreversible on the things done in the body.   To add
emphasis to the notion of finality in the work of

Christ's life on earth, the Apostle uses the passive verb,
" was offered." *   The offering, it is true, was made by
Christ Himself.   But here the deed is more emphatic
than the Doer: "He was offered once for all."   The
result of the offering is also emphasised: "He was
offered *so as* † to lift up sins, like a heavy burden,
and bear them away for ever."   Even the word
"many" is not to be slurred over.   It too indicates
that the work of Christ was final; for the sins of *many*
have been put away.

What will be the judgment on Christ's one redemptive death?   Has it been a failure?   The answer is
that His death and His coming into the judgment have
a closer relation to men than mere similarity.   He
entered into the presence of God as a sin-offering.   He
will be proved, at His second appearing, to have put
away sin.   For He will appear then apart from ‡ sin.
God will pronounce that Christ's blood has been
accepted, and that His work has been finished.   His
acquittal will be the acquittal of those whose sins He
bare in His body on the tree.

Nor will His appearing be now long delayed.   It
was already the end of the ages when He first appeared.
Therefore look out for Him with eager expectancy §
and upward gaze.   For He will be once again actually

---

* προσενεχθείς (ix. 28).   † εἰς.   ‡ χωρίς.   § ἀπεκδεχομένοις.

beheld by human eyes, and; the vision will be unto salvation.

We must not fail to note that, when the Apostle speaks in this passage of Christ's being once offered, he refers to His death. The analogy between men and Christ breaks down completely if the death of Christ was not the offering for sin. Faustus Socinus revived the Nestorian doctrine that our author represents the earthly life and death of Jesus as a moral preparation for the priesthood which was conferred upon Him at His ascension to the right hand of God. The bearing of this interpretation of the Epistle on the Socinian doctrine generally is plain. A moral preparation there undoubtedly was, as the Apostle has shown in the second chapter. But if Christ was not Priest on earth, His death was not an atoning sacrifice. If He was not Priest, He was not Victim. Moreover, if He fills the office of Priest in heaven only, His priesthood cannot involve suffering and, therefore, cannot be an atonement. But the view is inconsistent with the Apostle's express statement that, " as it is appointed unto men once to die, so Christ was once offered." Of course, we cannot acquiesce in the opposite view that His death was Christ's only priestly act, and that His life in heaven is such a state of exaltation as excludes the possibility of priestly service. For He is " a Minister of the sanctuary, and of the true taber-

nacle, which the Lord pitched, not man." *   The death
of Christ was a distinct act of priestly service.   But it
must not be separated from His entering into heaven.
Aaron received into his hands the blood of the newly
slain victim, and immediately carried the smoking
blood into the holiest place.   The act of offering the
blood before God was as necessary to constitute the
atonement as the previous act of slaying the animal.
Hence it is that the shedding and the sprinkling of
the blood are spoken of as one and the same action.
Christ, in like manner, went into the true holiest
through His death.   Any other way of entering heaven
than through a sacrificial death would have destroyed
the priestly character of His heavenly life.   But His
death would have been insufficient.   He must offer
His blood and appear in the presence of God for us.
To give men access unto God was the ultimate purpose
of redemption.   He must, therefore, consecrate through
the veil of His flesh—a new and living way by which
we may come unto God through Him.

Must we, therefore, say that Christ entered the
holiest place at His death, not at His ascension?
Does the Apostle refer only to the entrance of the
soul into the invisible world?   The question is not
an easy one.   If the Apostle means the Ascension,

* Chap. viii. 2,

what doctrinal use does he make of the interval
between the Crucifixion and the Ascension? Many of
the fathers are evidently at a loss to know what to
make of this interval. They think the Divine person,
as well as the human soul, of Christ was conveyed
to Hades to satisfy what they call the law of death.
Does the Epistle to the Hebrews pass over in silence
the descent into Hades and the resurrection? On the
other hand, if our author means that Christ entered the
holiest place immediately at His death, we are met by
the difficulty that He leaves the holiest, to return
finally at His ascension, whereas the Apostle has
argued that Christ differs from the high-priests under
the former covenant in that He does not enter
repeatedly. Much of the confusion has arisen from
the tendency of theologians, under the influence of
Augustine, to construct their systems exclusively on
the lines of St. Paul. In his Epistles atonement is a
forensic conception. "Through one act of righteousness the free gift came unto all men to the justification
of life." * Consequently the death of Christ is contrasted with His present life. "For the death that He
died, He died unto sin once; but the life that He liveth,
He liveth unto God." † But our author does not put
his doctrine in a Pauline framework. Instead of forensic

---

* Rom. v. 18,   † Rom. vi. 10.

notions, we meet with terms pertaining to ritual and priesthood. What St. Paul speaks of as law is, in his language, a covenant, and what is designated justification in the Epistle to the Romans appears here as sanctification. Conscience is purified; the worshipper is perfected. The entering of the high-priest into the holiest place is as prominent as the slaying of the victim. These are two distinct, but inseparable, parts of one priestly action. All that lies between is ignored. It is as if it were not. Christ entered into the holiest through His death and ascension to the right hand of the Majesty. But the initial and the ultimate stages of the act must not be put asunder. Nothing comes between. Our author elsewhere speaks of Christ's resurrection as a historical fact.* But His resurrection does not form a distinct notion in the idea of His entrance into the holiest place.

The Apostle has spoken of the former covenant with surprising severity, not to say harshness. It was the law of a carnal commandment; it has been set aside because of its weakness and unprofitableness; it has grown old and waxed aged; it was nigh unto vanishing away. His austere language will compare with St. Paul's description of heathenism as a bondage to weak and beggarly elements.

---

* Chap. xiii. 20.

The root of all the mischief was unreality. Our
author brings his argument to a close by contrasting
the shadow and the substance, the unavailing sacrifices
of the Law, which could only renew the remembrance
of sins, and the sacrifice of the Son, which has fulfilled
the will of God.

The Law had only a shadow.*   He is careful not to
say that the Law was itself but a shadow.   On the
contrary, the very promise includes that God will put
His laws in the heart and write them upon the mind.
This was one of " the good things to come."   Endless
repetition of sacrifice after sacrifice year by year in a
weary round of ceremonies only made it more and
more evident that men were walking in a vain show
and disquieting themselves in vain.   The Law was holy,
righteous, and good ;   but the manifestation of its
nature in sacrifices was unreal, like the dark outline
of an object that breaks the stream of light.   Nothing
more substantial, as a revelation of God's moral character, was befitting or possible in that stage of human
development, when the purposes of His grace also not
seldom found expression in dreams of the night and
apparitions of the day.

To prove the unreal nature of these ever-recurring
sacrifices, the writer argues that otherwise they

---

* Chap. x. 1.

would have ceased to be offered, inasmuch as the worshippers, if they had been once really cleansed from their guilt, would have had no more conscience of sins.* The reasoning is very remarkable. It is not that God would have ceased to require sacrifices, but that the worshipper would have ceased to offer them. It implies that, when a sufficient atonement for sin has been offered to God, the sinner knows it is sufficient, and, as the result, has peace of conscience. The possibility of a pardoned sinner still fearing and doubting does not seem to have occurred to the Apostle. One difference apparently between the saints under the Old Testament and believers under the New is the joyful assurance of pardon which the latter receive, whereas the former were all their lifetime subject to bondage from fear of death, and that although in the one case the sacrifice was offered by the worshipper himself through the priest, but in the latter case by Another, even Christ, on his behalf. And we must not ask the Apostle such questions as these : Are we not in danger of deceiving ourselves ? How is the assurance created and kept alive ? Does it spring spontaneously in the heart, or is it the acceptance of the authoritative absolution of God's ministers ? Such problems were not thought of when the Epistle to the Hebrews was

---

* Chap. x. 2.

written. They belong to a later and more subjective
state of mind. To men who cannot leave off introspection and forget themselves in the joy of a new faith,
the Apostle's argument will have little force and
perhaps less meaning.

If the sacrifices were unreal, why, we naturally
inquire, were they continually repeated? The answer
is that there were two sides to the sacrificial rites of
the old covenant. On the one hand, they were, like
the heathen gods, "nothings;" on the other, their
empty shadowiness itself fitted them to be a Divinely
appointed means to call sins to remembrance. They
represented on the one side the invincible, though
always baffled, effort of natural conscience. For conscience was endeavouring to purify itself from a sense
of guilt. But God also had a purpose in awakening
and disciplining conscience. The worshipper sought to
appease conscience through sacrifice, and God, by the
same sacrifice, proclaimed that reconciliation had not
been effected. The Apostle's judgment on the subject *
is not different from St. Paul's answer to the question,
What then is the Law? "It was added because of
transgressions. . . . The Scripture hath shut up all
things under sin. . . . We were kept in ward under
the Law. . . . We were held in bondage under the

---

* Chap. x. 3.

rudiments of the world." * In allusion to this idea,
that the sacrifices were instituted by God in order to
renew the remembrance of sins every year, Christ said,
" Do this in remembrance of *Me*,"—of Him Who hath
put away sins by the sacrifice of Himself.

Such then was the shadow, at once unreal and dark.
In contrast to it, the Apostle designates the substance
as " the very image of the objects."   Instead of repeat-
ing the indefinite expression " good things to come,"
he speaks of them as " objects,"† individually distinct,
substantial, true.   The image‡ of a thing is the full
manifestation of its inmost essence, in the same sense
in which St. Paul says that the Son of God's love, in
Whom we have our redemption, the forgiveness of our
sins, is the image of the invisible God. §   Indeed, it is
extremely questionable whether our author too does
not refer allusively to the same truth.   For, in the
verses that follow, he contrasts with the sacrifices of
the former covenant the coming of Jesus Christ into
the world to accomplish the work which they had failed
to do. ‖   When the blood of bulls and goats could not
take away sin, inasmuch as it was an unreal atonement,
God prepared a body for His own eternal Son.   The
Son responded to the Divine summons and, in accordance with the prophecies of Scripture concerning Him,

---

* Gal. iii. 19—iv. 3.   ‡ εἰκόνα.

† πραγμάτων (x. 1).   § Col. i. 14, 15,   ‖ Chap. x. 5 sqq.

came from heaven to earth to give Himself as the
sufficient sacrifice for sin.　The contrast, as heretofore,
is between the vanity of animal sacrifices and the
greatness of the Son, Who offered Himself.　His
assumption of humanity had for its ultimate end to
enable the Son to do the will of God.　The gracious
purpose of God is to forgive sin, and this was accomplished by the infinite humiliation of the infinite Son.
God's will was to sanctify us ; that is, to remove our
guilt.*　We have actually been thus sanctified through
the one offering of the body of Jesus Christ.　The
sacrifices of the Law are taken out of the way in order
to establish the sacrifice of the Son. †

It will be observed that the Apostle is not contrasting sacrifice and obedience.　His meaning is not
precisely the same as the prophet Samuel's : that " to
obey is better than sacrifice, and to hearken than the
fat of rams." ‡　It is perfectly true that the sacrifice of
the Son involved obedience,—a conscious, deliberate,
willing obedience, which the beasts to be slain in sacrifice could not offer.　The idea pervades these verses,
as an atmosphere.　But it is not the idea expressed.
The dominant thoughts of the passage are the greatness of the Person Who obeyed and the greatness of
the sacrifice from which His obedience did not shrink.

---

* Chap. x. 10.　　　† Chap. x. 9.　　　‡ I Sam. xv. 22.

The Son is here represented as existing and acting apart from His human nature.*   He comes into the world, and is not originated in the world.   The Christology of the Epistle to the Hebrews is identical in this vital point with that of St. Paul.   The purpose of the Son's coming is already formed.   He comes to offer His body, and we have been taught in a previous chapter that He did this with an eternal spirit.†   For the will of God means our sanctification, in the meaning attached to the word "sanctification" in this Epistle, the removal of guilt, the forgiveness of sins. But the fulfilment of this gracious will of God demands a sacrifice, even a sacrificial death, and that not the death of beasts, but the infinite self-sacrifice and obedience unto death of the Son of God.   This is implied in the expression "the offering of the body of Jesus Christ." ‡

The superstructure of argument has been raised. Christ as High-priest has been proved to be superior to the high-priests of the former covenant.   It remains only to lay the topstone in its place.   This brings us back to our starting point.   Jesus Christ, the eternal High-priest, is for ever King.   For the priests under the Law stand while they perform the duties of their

---

* Chap. x. 7.   † Chap. ix. 14.   ‡ Chap. x. 10.

ministry.*   They stand because they are only priests.
But Christ has taken His seat, as King, on the right
hand of God. †   They offer the same sacrifices, which
can never take away sins, and wait, and wait, but in
vain.   Though they are priests of the true God, yet
they wait, like the priests of Baal, from morning until
midday is past and until the time of the offering of the
evening sacrifice.   But there is neither voice nor any
to answer.   Christ also waits, but not to renew an
ineffectual sacrifice.   He waits eagerly ‡ to receive
from God the reward of His effective sacrifice in the
subjugation of His enemies.   The priests under the
Law had no enemies.   Their persons were sacred.
They incurred no hatred, inspired no love.   Our High-
priest goes out to war, the most hated, the most loved,
of all captains of men.

The foundation of this kingly power is in two things :
first, He has perfected men for ever by His one offering ; second, He has put the law of God into the hearts
of His people.   The final conclusion is that the sacrifices of the Law have passed away, because they are no
longer needed.   " For where there is forgiveness, there
is no more an offering for sin."

---

* Chap. x. 11.   † Chap. x. 13.   ‡ ἐκδεχόμενος (x. 13).

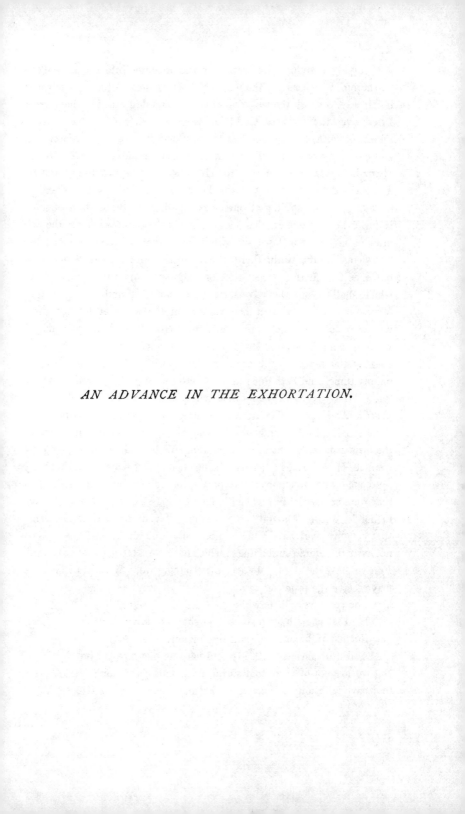

AN ADVANCE IN THE EXHORTATION.

" Having therefore, brethren, boldness to enter into the holy place by the blood of Jesus, by the way which He dedicated for us, a new and living way, through the veil, that is to say, His flesh ; and having a great Priest over the house of God ; let us draw near with a true heart in fulness of faith, having our hearts sprinkled from an evil conscience, and our body washed with pure water : let us hold fast the confession of our hope that it waver not ; for He is faithful that promised : and let us consider one another to provoke unto love and good works; not forsaking the assembling of ourselves together, as the custom of some is, but exhorting one another ; and so much the more, as ye see the day drawing nigh.   For if we sin wilfully after that we have received the knowledge of the truth, there remaineth no more a sacrifice for sins, but a certain fearful expectation of judgment, and a fierceness of fire which shall devour the adversaries.   A man that hath set at nought Moses' law dieth without compassion on the word of two or three witnesses : of how much sorer punishment, think ye, shall he be judged worthy, who hath trodden under foot the Son of God, and hath counted the blood of the covenant, wherewith he was sanctified, an unholy thing, and hath done despite unto the Spirit of grace ?   For we know Him that said, Vengeance belongeth unto Me.   I will recompense.   And again, The Lord shall judge His people.   It is a fearful thing to fall into the hands of the living God.   But call to remembrance the former days, in which, after ye were enlightened, ye endured a great conflict of sufferings ;   partly, being made a gazing-stock both by reproaches and afflictions ; and partly, becoming partakers with them that were so used.   For ye both had compassion on them that were in bonds, and took joyfully the spoiling of your possessions, knowing that ye yourselves have a better possession and an abiding one.   Cast not away therefore your boldness, which hath great recompense of reward. For ye have need of patience, that, having done the will of God, ye may receive the promise.

For yet a very little while,

He that cometh shall come, and shall not tarry.

But My righteous one shall live by faith :

And if he shrink back, My soul hath no pleasure in him.

But we are not of them that shrink back unto perdition ; but of them that have faith unto the saving of the soul."—HEB. x. 19—39 (R.V.).

CHAPTER IX.

AN ADVANCE IN THE EXHORTATION.

THE argument is closed. Christ is the eternal
Priest and King, and every rival priesthood or
kingship must come to an end. This is the truth won
by the Apostle's original and profound course of
reasoning. But he has in view practical results. He
desires to confirm the Hebrew Christians in their
allegiance to Christ. We shall be better able to understand the precise bearing of his exhortation if we
compare it with the appeal previously made to his
readers in the earlier chapters of the Epistle.* At the
very outset he plunged into the midst of his subject
and proved that Jesus Christ is Son of God and representative Man. The union in Christ of these two
qualifications constituted Him a great High-priest. He
is able to succour the tempted ; He is faithful as a Son,
Who is set over the house of God ; He has experienced
the bitter humiliation of life , He is perfected as our

---

* Chaps. ii. i—5; iii. 1, 6 ; iv. 11, 16 ; vi.

Saviour, and has passed through the heavens. The exhortation, based on these truths, is that we must lay fast hold of our confidence.

Then come the big wave, the hesitation to face it, the allegory of Melchizedek, the appeal to the prophet Jeremiah, the comparison between the old covenant and the new. But the argument triumphs and advances. Jesus not only is a great High-priest, but this is interpreted as meaning that He is Priest and King, and that His priesthood and power will never pass away. Their eternal duration involves the setting aside of every other priesthood, the destruction of every opposing force. Christ has entered into the true holiest place and enthroned Himself on the mercy-seat.

This being so, the Apostle no longer urges his readers to be confident. He now appeals to them as having confidence,* in virtue of the blood of Jesus, so that they tarry not in the precincts, but enter themselves into the holiest. The high-priest alone dared enter under the former covenant, and he approached with fear and trembling, lest he also, like others before him, should fall down dead in the presence of God. The exhortation now is, not to confidence, but to sincerity.† Let their confidence become more objective. They

---

* Chap. x. 19. † μετὰ ἀληθινῆς καρδίας (x. 22).

had the boasting of hope. Let them seek the silent,
unboasting assurance that is grounded on faith, on the
realisation of the invisible. Instead of believing because they hoped, let them hope because they believed.
In the earlier chapters the exhortation rested mainly
on what Jesus was as Son over God's house. Now,
however, the Apostle speaks of Him as a *great* * Priest
over God's house. His authority over the Church
springs, not only from His relation to God, but also
from His relation to men. He is King of His Church
because He prays for it and blesses it. Through His
priesthood our hearts are cleansed by the sprinkling of
His blood from the consciousness of sin.† But this
blessing of the individual believer is now closely connected by the Apostle with the idea of the Church,
over which Christ is King in virtue of His priesthood
on its behalf. In addition to the cleansing of our
hearts from an evil conscience, our bodies have been
washed with pure water. The Apostle alludes primarily in both clauses to the rite of priestly consecration.
" Moses brought Aaron and his sons, and washed
them with water." He also " took of the blood which
was upon the altar and sprinkled it upon Aaron, and
upon his garments, and upon his sons, and upon his
sons' garments with him, and sanctified Aaron, and

---

* μέγαν (x. 21).   † ἀπὸ συνειδήσεως πονηρᾶς (x. 22).

his garments, and his sons, and his sons' garments
with him." * The meaning of our author seems
certainly to be that the worshippers have the privilege
of the high-priest himself. They lose their priestly
character only in the more excellent glory and greatness of that High-priest through Whom they have
received their priesthood. In comparison with Him,
they are but humble worshippers, and He alone
is Priest. In contrast to the world around them, they
also are priests of God. But the words of the
Apostle contain another allusion. Both clauses refer
to baptism. The mention of washing the "body"
renders it, we think, unquestionable that baptism is
meant. But baptism is not here said to be the antitype
of the priestly consecration of the old covenant.
One rite cannot be the type of another rite, which
is itself an external action. The solution of this apparent difficulty is simply that *both* clauses together
mean baptism, which is invariably represented in
the New Testament as much more than an outward
rite. The external act may be performed without
its being a true baptism. For the meaning of baptism
is the forgiveness of sin, the cleansing of the heart or
innermost consciousness from guilt, and the reception
of the absolved sinner into the Church of God.

* Lev. viii. 6, 30.

"Christ loved the Church, and gave Himself up for it, that He might sanctify it, having cleansed it by the washing of water with the word." *

In an earlier chapter our author told his readers that they were the house of God if they held fast their confidence. He does not repeat it. The Church consciousness *has* sprung up within them. They were previously taught to look steadfastly at Jesus as the Apostle and High-priest of their confession.† They are now urged to look as steadfastly at one another as fellow-confessors of the same Apostle and High-priest, and to sharpen one another's love and activity even to the point of jealousy.‡ In the earlier exhortation no mention was made of the Church assemblies. Here prominence is given them. Importance is attached to the words of encouragement addressed at these gatherings of believers. Christian habits were at this time forming and consolidating into customs of the Church. Occasional and eccentric manifestations of the religious life and temperament were yielding to the slow, normal growth of **true vitality.** As faithfulness in frequenting the **Church** assemblies began to rank among the foremost virtues, unfaithfulness would, by force of contrast, harden into habitual neglect of the house of prayer: "As the custom of some is." §

---

* Eph. v. 26.   ‡ εἰς παροξυσμόν (x. 24).
† Chap. iii. 1.   § ἔθος (x. 25).

The chief of all reasons for exhorting the readers to
habitual attendance on the Church assemblies the
writer of the Epistle finds in the expectation of the
Lord's speedy return.   They could see for themselves
that the day was at hand.   The signs of the Son of
man's coming were multiplying and thrusting themselves on the notice of the Church.   Perhaps the voice
of Joshua, the son of Hanan, had already been heard
in the streets, exclaiming, "Woe to Jerusalem!"   The
holy city was plainly doomed.   But Christ will come to
His Church, not to individuals.   He will not be found
in the wilderness, nor in the inner chambers.   "As the
lightning cometh forth from the east, and is seen even
unto the west, so shall be the coming of the Son of
man."*

The day of Christ is a day of judgment.   The two
meanings of the word "day,"—day in contrast to
night, and day as a fixed time for the transaction of
public business,—coalesce in the New Testament usage.
The second idea seems to have gradually superseded
the former.

The author proceeds to unfold the dreadful character
of this day of judgment.   Here, again, the precise
force of his declarations will best appear by comparison with the warnings of the first part of the Epistle
in reference to the sin and to the punishment.

* Matt. xxiv. 27.

First, the sin referred to here has a wider range than the transgression spoken of in the second chapter. For there he mentions the special sin of neglecting so great salvation. But in the present passage his words seem to imply that rejection of Christ has given birth to a progeny of evil through the self-abandonment of those who wilfully persist in sinning, as if from reckless bravado.* The special guilt, too, of rejecting Christ is here painted in darker hues. For in the earlier passage it is indifference; here it is contempt. In the former case it is ingratitude to a merciful Saviour; in the latter it is treason against the majesty of God's own Son. "To trample under foot" means to desecrate. Christ is the holy High-priest of God, and is now ministering in the true holiest place. Therefore to choose Judaism, with its dead rites, and to reject the living Christ, is no longer the action of a holy zeal for God's house. Quite the reverse. The sanctuary of Judaism has been shorn of its glory, and its sacredness transferred to the despised Nazarene. To tread under foot the Son of God is to trample with revel rout on the hallowed floor of the holiest place. Further, the Apostle's former warnings contained no allusion to the covenant. Now he reminds his readers that they have been sanctified—that is, cleansed from

---

* ἐκουσίως (x. 26)

guilt—through the blood of the covenant.   Is the cleansing blood itself unclean ?   Shall we deem the reeking gore of a slain beast or the grey ashes of a burnt heifer holy, and consider the blood of the Christ, Who with an eternal spirit offered Himself without spot to God, unholy and defiling ? *   Moreover, that eternal spirit in the Son of God is a spirit of grace † towards men. But His infinite compassion is spurned.   And thus the Apostle brings us once more ‡ in sight of the hopeless character of cynicism.

Second, the punishment is partly negative.   A sacrifice for sins is no more left to men who have spurned the sacrifice of the Son.§   Here again we notice an advance in the thought.   The Apostle told his readers before that it is impossible to renew to repentance those who crucify afresh the Son of God and put Him to an open shame.   But the impossibility consists in hardness of heart and spiritual blindness.   The result also is subjective,—they cannot repent.   He now adds the impossibility of finding another propitiation than the offering of Christ or of finding in His offering a different kind of propitiation, seeing that He is the final revelation of God's forgiving grace.   Then, further, the punishment has a positive side.   After hardness of heart comes stinging remorse, arising from a vague,

---

* Chap. x. 29.

† πνεῦμα τῆς χάριτος.

‡ See chap. vi. 6.

§ Chap. x. 26.

but on that account all the more fearful, expectation
of the judgment.   The abject terror is amply justified.
For the fury* of a fire, already kindling around the
doomed city, warns the Hebrew backsliders that the
Christ so wilfully scoffed at is at the door.   Observe
the contrast.   The law of Moses is on occasion set
aside.   The matter is almost private.   Only two or
three persons witnessed it.†   Its evil influence did not
spread, and when the criminal was led out to be stoned
to death, they who passed by went their way unheed-
ing.   The Christ of God is put to an open shame ; ‡ the
covenant, for ever established on the sure foundation
of God's oath and Christ's death, and the spirit of all
grace that filled the heart of Christ are mocked.   Of
how much sorer punishment shall Christ at His speedy
coming deem the scorner worthy ?   The answer is left
by the Apostle to his readers.   They knew with Whom
they had to do.§   It was not with angels, the swift
messengers and flaming ministers of His power.   It
was not with Moses, who himself exceedingly feared and
quaked. ‖   It was not with the blind pressure of fate.
They had to do with the living God Himself directly.
He will lay upon them His living hand,—the hand that
might and, if they had not spurned it, would have
protected and saved.   Retribution descends swift and

---

* ζῆλος (x. 27).　　† Chap. x. 28.　　‡ παραδειγματίζοντας (vi. 6).
§ Chap. iii. 12.　　　　　　‖ Chap. xii. 21.

resistless.   It can only be likened to a sudden falling
into the very hands of a waiting avenger.*   He will
not entrust the work of vengeance to another.   No
extraneous agent shall come between the smiting hand
and the heart that burns with the anger of the sincere
against the false, of the compassionate against the
pitiless.   Does not Scripture teach that the Lord will
execute judgment on behalf of His people? †   If on
behalf of His people, will He not enter into judgment
for His Son?

From the terrible expectation of future judgment the
Apostle turns away, to recall to his readers the grounds
of hope supplied by their steadfastness in the past.   He
has already spoken of their work and the love which
they had shown in ministering to the saints.‡   God's
justice would not forget their brotherly kindness.   Now,
however, His purpose in bidding them remember the
former days is something different.   He writes to con-
vince them that they needed no other and greater
confidence to face the future than had carried them
triumphantly through conflicts in days of yore.   They
had endured sufferings; let them conquer their own
indifference and put away their cynicism with the lofty
disdain of earnest faith.   The courage that could do
the former can also do the latter.

---

* ἐμπεσεῖν.   † Deut. xxxii. 36.   ‡ Chap. vi. 10.

From the first break of day in their souls* they had
felt the confidence of men who walk, not in darkness,
not knowing whither they go and fearing to take
another step, but in the light, so that they trod firmly
and stepped boldly onward. Their confidence was
based on conviction and understanding of truth. For
that reason it inspired them with the courage of
athletes,† when they had to endure also the shame of
the arena. Made a gazing-stock to a scoffing theatre,
they had not turned pale at the roar of the wild
beasts. Instead of tamely submitting, they had turned
their sufferings into a veritable contest against the
world, and maintained the conflict long.‡ Taunted by
the spectators, torn by the lions, reproaches and
afflictions alike had been ineffectual to break their
spirit. When they witnessed the prolonged tortures
of their brethren whose Christian life was one martyrdom,§ they had not shrunk from the like usage. They
had pitied the brethren in prisons and visited them.
They had taken joyfully the spoiling of their substance,
knowing that now they had themselves, ‖ as a better
and an abiding possession. If they had lost the world,
they had gained for themselves their souls.¶ As true

---

* φωτισθέντας (x. 32).
† ἄθλησιν.
‡ πολλήν.

§ οὕτως ἀναστρεφομένων (x. 33).
‖ Reading ἑαυτούς (x. 34).
¶ εἰς περιποίησιν (x. 39).

13

athletes, therefore, let them not throw away * their
sword, which is no other than their old, undaunted
confidence. There was none like that sword. Their
victory was assured. Their reward would be, not the
plaudits of the fickle onlookers, but the fulfilment of
God's promise to Abraham. They had need of endurance, because in enduring they were doing the will
of God. But the Deliverer would be with them in a
twinkling.† He had delayed His chariot wheels, but
He would delay no more. Hear ye not His voice? It is
He that speaks in the words of the prophet, "Those
whom I deny will perish out of the way. But I have
My righteous ones ‡ here and there, unseen by the
world, and out of their faith will be wrought for them
eternal life. But let even Mine own beware of lowering
sail. My soul will have no delight even in him if he
draws back."

The Apostle reflects on the words of Christ in the
prophecy of Habakkuk. But he has an assured hope
that he and his readers would repudiate the thought
of drawing back. They were men of faith, bent on
winning § the prize of the high calling of God in Christ
Jesus; and the prize would be their own souls.
May we not conjecture that the Apostle's fervid appeal
prevailed with the Christians within the doomed city

---

* μὴ ἀποβάλητε.

† μικρὸν ὅσον ὅσον (x. 37).

‡ Reading μου (x. 38).

§ περιποίησιν (x. 39).

" to break the last bands of patriotism and superstition which attached them to the Temple and the altar, and proclaim themselves missionaries of the new faith, without a backward glance of lingering reminiscence " ? *

* Dean Merivale, *Romans under the Empire,* chap. lix.

FAITH AN ASSURANCE AND A PROOF.

" Now faith is the assurance of things hoped for, the proving of things not seen. For therein the elders had witness borne to them. By faith we understand that the worlds have been framed by the word of God so that what is seen hath not been made out of things which do appear."—HEB. xi. 1—3 (R.V.).

CHAPTER X.

FAITH AN ASSURANCE AND A PROOF.

IT is often said that one of the greatest difficulties in the Epistle to the Hebrews is to discover any real connection of ideas between the author's general purpose in the previous discussion and the splendid record of faith in the eleventh chapter. The rhetorical connection is easy to trace. His utterances throughout have been incentives to confidence. "Let us hold fast our confession." "Let us draw near with boldness unto the throne of grace." "Show diligence unto the full assurance of hope." "Cast not away your boldness." Any of these exhortations would sufficiently describe the Apostle's practical aim from the beginning of the Epistle. But he has just cited the words of Habakkuk, and the prophet speaks of faith. How, then, does the prophet's declaration that the righteous man of God will escape death by his faith bear on the Apostle's arguments or help his strong appeals? The first verse of the eleventh chapter is the reply. Faith *is* assurance with emphasis on the verb.

But this is only a rhetorical connection, or at best a justification of the use the author has made of the prophet's words. Indeed, he has already in several places identified confidence with faith, and the opposite of confidence with unbelief. "Take heed lest there be in any one of you an evil heart of unbelief; . . . for we are become partakers of Christ if we hold fast the beginning of our confidence firm unto the end." * "They could not enter in because of unbelief; . . . let us therefore give diligence to enter into that rest, that no man fall after the same example of disobedience." † "Be not sluggish, but imitators of them who through faith and patience inherit the promises."‡ "Having therefore boldness to enter into the holy place, . . . let us draw near with a true heart in fulness of faith." §

Why, therefore, does the author formally state that faith is confidence? The difficulty is a real one. We must suppose that, when this Epistle was written, the word "faith" was already a well-known and almost technical term among Christians. We infer as much as this also from St. James's careful and stringent correction of abuses in the application of the word. It is unnecessary to say who was the first to perceive the vital importance of faith in the life and theology

* Chap. iii. 12.
† Chaps. iii. 19 ; iv. 11.
‡ Chap. vi. 12.
§ Chap. x. 19.

of Christianity. But in the preaching of St. Paul faith is trust in a personal Saviour, and trust is the condition and instrument of salvation. Faith, thus represented, is the opposite of works. Such a doctrine was liable to abuse, and has been abused to the utter subversion of morality on the one hand and to the extinction of all unselfish greatness of soul on the other. Not, most certainly, that St. Paul himself was one-sided in teaching or in character. To him Christ is a heavenly ideal: "The Lord is the Spirit;" and to him the believer is the spiritual man, who has the moral intellect of Christ.* But it must be confessed—and the history of the Church abundantly proves the truth of the statement—that the good news of eternal salvation on the sole condition of trust in Christ is one of the easiest of all true doctrines to be fatally abused. The Epistle of St. James and the Epistle to the Hebrews seem to have been written to meet this danger. The former represents faith as the inner life of the spirit, the fountain of all active goodness. "Faith, if it have not works, is dead in itself. Yea, a man will say, Thou hast faith, and I have works; show me thy faith apart from thy works, and I by my works will show thee my faith."† St. James contends against the earliest phases of Antinomianism. He reconciles faith

---

* 2 Cor. iii. 17 ; 1 Cor. ii. 16. † James ii. 17, 18.

and morality, and maintains that the highest morality springs out of faith. The writer of the Epistle to the Hebrews contends against legalism,—the proud, self-satisfied, indifferent, hard, slothful, contemptuous, cynical spirit, which is quite as truly and as often an abuse of the doctrine of salvation through faith. It is the terrible plague of those Churches which have never risen above individualism. When men are told that the whole of religion consists in securing the soul's eternal safety, and that this salvation is made sure once for all by a moment's trust in Christ, their after-life will harden into a worldliness, not gross and sensual, but pitiless and deadening. They will put on the garb of religious decorum; but the inner life will be eaten by the canker of covetousness and self-righteous pride. These are the men described in the sixth chapter of our Epistle, who have, after a fashion, repented and believed, but whose religion has no recuperative power, let alone the growth and richness of deep vitality.

Our author addresses men whose spiritual life was thus imperilled. Their condition is not that of the heathen world in its agony of despair. He does not call his readers, in the words of St. Paul to the jailer at Philippi, to trust themselves into the hands of the Lord Jesus Christ, that they may be saved. Yet he too insists on faith. He is anxious to show them that he is not preaching another gospel, but unfolding the meaning of the same conception of faith, which is the central principle of the Gospel revealed at the first by Christ to their fathers, and applied to the wants of the heathen by the Apostle of the Gentiles.

If so, it goes without saying that the writer does not intend to give a scholastic definition of faith. The New Testament is not the book in which to seek formal definitions. For his present purpose we require only to know that, whatever else faith includes, confidence in reference to the objects of our hope must find a place in it. Faith bridges over the chasm between hope and the things hoped for. It saves us from building castles in the air or living in a fool's paradise. The phantoms of worldliness and the phantoms of religion (for they too exist) will not deceive us. In the course of his discussion in the Epistle the author has used three different words to set forth various sides of the same feeling of confidence. One refers to the freedom and boldness with which the confidence felt manifests its presence in words and action.* Another signifies the fulness of conviction with which the mind when confident is saturated.† The third word, which we have in the present passage, describes confidence as a reality, resting on an unshaken foundation, and

---

* παρρησία.   † πληροφορία,

contrasted with illusions.* He has urged Christians to boldness of action and fulness of conviction. Now he adds that faith is that boldness and that wealth of certitude in so far as they rest upon reality and truth.

We can now in some measure estimate the value of the Apostle's description of faith as an assurance concerning things hoped for, and apply it to give force to the exhortations of the Epistle. The evil heart of unbelief is the moral corruption of the man whose soul is steeped in sensual imaginations and never realises the things of the Spirit. They who came out of Egypt by Moses could not enter into rest because they did not descry, beyond the earthly Canaan, the rest of the spirit in God. Others inherit the promises, because on earth they lifted their hearts to the heavenly country. In short, the Apostle now tells his readers that the true source of Christian constancy and boldness is the realisation of the unseen world.

But faith is this assurance concerning things hoped for because it is a proof † of their existence, and of the existence of the unseen generally. The latter part of the verse is the broad foundation on which faith rests in all the rich variety of its meanings and practical applications. Here St. Paul, St. James, and the writer of the Epistle to the Hebrews meet in the unity of their

---

* ὑπόστασις. † ἔλεγχος.

conception. Whether men trust unto salvation, or develop their inner spiritual life, or enter into communion with God and lift the weapon of unflinching boldness in the Christian warfare, trust, character, confidence, all three derive their being and vitality from faith, as it demonstrates the existence of the unseen.

The Apostle's language is a seeming contradiction. Proof is usually supposed to dispense with faith and compel us to accept the inference drawn. He intentionally describes faith as occupying in reference to spiritual realities the place of demonstration. Faith in the unseen is itself a proof that the unseen world exists. It is so in two ways.

First, we trust our own moral instincts. Malebranche observes that our passions justify themselves. How much more is this true of intellect and conscience! In like manner, some men have firm confidence in a world of spiritual realities, which eye has not seen. This confidence is itself a proof to them. How do I know that I know? It is a philosopher's enigma. For us it may be sufficient to say that to know and to know that we know are one and the same act. How do we justify our faith in the unseen? The answer is similar. It is the same thing to trust and to trust our trust. Scepticism wins a cheap victory when it arraigns faith as a culprit caught in the very act of stealing the forbidden fruit of paradise But when, like a guilty thing, faith blushes for its want of logic, its only refuge is to look in the face of the unseen Father. He who has most faith in his own spiritual instincts will have the strongest faith in God. To trust God is to trust ourselves. To doubt ourselves is to doubt God. We must add that there is a sense in which trust in God means distrust of self.

Second, faith fastens directly on God Himself. We believe in God because we impose implicit confidence in our own moral nature. With equal truth we may also say that we believe all else because we believe in God. Faith in God Himself immediately and personally is the proof that the promises are true, that our life on earth is linked to a life above, that patient well-doing will have its reward, that no good deed can be in vain, and ten thousand other thoughts and hopes that sustain the drooping spirit in hours of conflict. It may well happen that some of these truths are legitimate inferences from premises, or it may be that a calculation of probabilities is in favour of their truth. But faith trusts itself upon them because they are worthy of God. Sometimes the silence of God is enough, if an aspiration of the soul is felt to be such that it became Him to implant it and will be glorious in Him to reward the heaven-sent desire.

An instance of faith as a proof of the unseen is given

by our author in the third verse. We may paraphrase it thus : "By faith we know that the ages have been constructed by the word of God, and that even to this point of assurance : that the visible universe as a whole came not into being out of things that do appear."

The author began in the previous verse to unroll his magnificent record of the elders. But from the beginning men found themselves in the presence of a mystery of the past before they received any promise as to the future. It is the mystery of creation. It has pressed heavily on men in all ages. The Apostle himself has felt its power, and speaks of it as a question which his readers and himself have faced. How do we know that the development of the ages had a beginning? If it had a beginning, how did it begin? The Apostle replies that we know it by faith. The revelation which we have received from God addresses itself to our moral perception and our confidence in God's moral nature. We have been taught that "in the beginning God created the heaven and the earth," and that "God said, Let there be light." * Faith demands this revelation. Is faith trust? That trust in God is our proof that the framework of the world was put together by His creative wisdom and power. Is faith the inner life of righteousness? Morality requires that our own

* Gen. i. 1, 3.

consciousness of personality and freedom should be derived from a Divine personality as the Originator of all things. Is faith communion with God? Those who pray know that prayer is an absolute necessity of their spiritual nature, and prayer lifts its voice to a living Father. Faith demonstrates to him who has it, though not to others, that the universe has come to its present form, not by an eternal evolution of matter, but by the action of God's creative energy.

The somewhat peculiar form of the clause seems certainly to suggest that the Apostle ascribes the origin of the universe, not only to a personal Creator, but to that personal Creator acting through the ideas of His own mind. "The visible came into being, not out of things that appear." We catch ourselves waiting till he finishes the sentence with the words, "but out of things that do not appear." Most expositors fight shy of the inference and explain it away by alleging that the negative has been misplaced.* But is it not true that the universe is the manifestation of thought in the unity of the Divine purpose? This is the very notion required to complete the Apostle's statement concerning faith as a proof. If faith demonstrates, it acts on principles. If God is personal, those principles are ideas, thoughts, purposes, of the Divine mind.

---

* As if μὴ ἐκ φαινομένων were for ἐκ μὴ φαινομένων.

So long, therefore, as our spiritual nature can trust, can unfold a morality, can pray, the simple soul need not much bewail its want of logic and its loss of arguments. If the famous ontological argument for the being of God has been refuted, we shall not, on that account, tremble for the ark. We shall not lament though the argument from the watch has proved treacherous. Our God is not a mere infinite mechanician. Indeed, such a phrase is a contradiction in terms. A mechanician must be finite. He contrives, and as the result produces, not what is absolutely best, but what is the best possible under the circumstances and with the materials at his disposal. But if we have lost the mechanician, we have not lost the God that thinks. We have gained the perfectly righteous and perfectly good. His thoughts have manifested themselves in nature, in human freedom, in the incarnation of His Son, in the redemption of sinners. But the intellect that knows these things is the good heart of faith.

THE FAITH OF ABRAHAM.

"By faith Abraham, when he was called, obeyed to go out unto a place which he was to receive for an inheritance ; and he went out, not knowing whither he went. By faith he became a sojourner in the land of promise, as in a land not his own, dwelling in tents, with Isaac and Jacob, the heirs with him of the same promise : for he looked for the city which hath the foundations, whose Builder and Maker is God. By faith even Sarah herself received power to conceive seed when she was past age, since she counted Him faithful Who had promised : wherefore also there sprang of one, and him as good as dead, so many as the stars of heaven in multitude, and as the sand, which is by the sea-shore, innumerable. These all died in faith, not having received the promises, but having seen them and greeted them from afar, and having confessed that they were strangers and pilgrims on the earth. For they that say such things make it manifest that they are seeking after a country of their own. And if indeed they had been mindful of that country from which they went out, they would have had opportunity to return. But now they desire a better country, that is, a heavenly : wherefore God is not ashamed of them, to be called their God : for He hath prepared for them a city. By faith Abraham, being tried, offered up Isaac : yea, he that had gladly received the promises was offering up his only-begotten son ; even he to whom it was said, In Isaac shall thy seed be called : accounting that God is able to raise up, even from the dead ; from whence he did also in a parable receive him back."—HEB. xi. 8—19(R.V.).

CHAPTER XI.

THE FAITH OF ABRAHAM.

WE have learned that faith is the proof of the unseen. We must not exclude even from this clause the other thought that faith is an assurance of things hoped for. It is not stated, but it is implied. The conception of a personal God requires only to be unfolded in order to yield a rich harvest of hope. The author proceeds to show that by faith the elders had witness borne to them in God's confession of them and great rewards. He recounts the achievements of a long line of believers, who as they went handed the light from one to another. In them is the true unity of religion and revelation from the beginning. For the poor order of high-priests the writer substitutes the glorious succession of faith.

We choose for the subject of this chapter the faith of Abraham. But we shall not dismiss in silence the faith of Abel, Enoch, and Noah. The paragraph in which Abraham's deeds are recorded will most naturally divide itself into three comparisons between their faith

and his.   We venture to think that this was in the
writer's mind and determined the form of the passage.
From the eighth to the tenth verse the Apostle compares Abraham's faith with that of Noah ; after a short
episode concerning Sarah, he compares Abraham's faith
with Enoch's, from the thirteenth verse to the six-
teenth ; then, down to the nineteenth verse, he
compares Abraham's faith with that of Abel.   Noah's
faith appeared in an act of obedience, Enoch's in a
life of fellowship with God, Abel's in his more
excellent sacrifice.   Abraham's faith manifested itself
in all these ways.   When he was called, he obeyed ;
when a sojourner, he desired a better country, that is,
a heavenly, and God was not ashamed to be called
his God ; being tried, he offered up Isaac.

Two points of surpassing worth in his faith suggest
themselves.   The one is largeness and variety of
experience ; the other is conquest over difficulties.
These are the constituents of a great saint.   Many
a good man will not become a strong spiritual character because his experience of life is too narrow.
Others, whose range is wide, fail to reach the higher
altitudes of saintliness because they have never been
called to pass through sore trials, or, if they have heard
the summons, have shrunk from the hardships.   Before
Abraham faith was both limited in its experience and
untested with heaven-sent difficulties.   Abraham's

religion was complex. His faith was "a perfect cube," and, presenting a face to every wind that blows, came victorious out of every trial.

Let us trace the comparisons.

First, Noah obeyed a Divine command when he built an ark to the saving of his house. He obeyed by faith. His eyes saw the invisible, and the vision kindled his hopes of being saved through the very waters that would destroy every living substance. But this was all. His faith acted only in one direction: he hoped to be saved. The Apostle Peter * compares his faith to the initial grace of those who seek baptism, and have only crossed the threshold of the spiritual life. It is true that he overcame one class of difficulties. He was not in bondage to the things of sense. He made provision for a future belied by present appearances. But the influence of the senses is not the greatest difficulty of the human spirit. As the lonely ship rode on the heaving waste of waters, all within was gladness and peace. No heaven-sent temptations tried the patriarch's faith. He overcame the trials that spring out of the earth but he knew not the anguish that rends the spirit like a lightning-stroke descending from God.

With Abraham it was otherwise. "He went out,

---

* 1 Peter iii. 20.

not knowing whither he went." *   He leaves his father's house and his father's gods.   He breaks for ever with the past, even before the future has been revealed to him.   The thoughts and feelings that had grown up with him from childhood are once for all put away. He has no sheltering ark to receive him.   A homeless wanderer, he pitches his tent to-day at the well, not knowing where his invisible guide may bid him stretch the cords on the morrow.   His departure from Ur of the Chaldees was a family migration.   But the writer of this Epistle, like Philo, describes it as the man's own personal obedience to a Divine call.   Submitting to God's will, possessed with the inspiration and courage of faith, obeying daily new intimations, he bends his steps this way or that, not knowing whither he goes.   True, he went right into the heart of the land of promise.   But, even in his own heritage, he became a sojourner, as in a land not his own.†   God " gave him none inheritance in it, no, not so much as to set his foot on." ‡   Possessor of all in promise, he purchased a sepulchre, which was the first ground he could call his own.   The cave of Machpelah was the small beginning of the fulfilment of God's promise, which the spirit of Abraham is even now receiving in a higher form.   It is still the same.   The bright dawn

---

* Chap. xi. 8.   † Chap. xi. 9.   ‡ Acts vii. 5.

of heaven often breaks upon the soul at an open grave.
But he journeyed on, and trusted.   For a time he and
Sarah only; afterwards Isaac with them; at last,
when Sarah had been laid to rest, Abraham, Isaac,
Jacob, the three together, held on bravely, sojourning
with aching hearts, but ever believing.   The Apostle
brings in the names of Isaac and Jacob, not to describe
their faith—this he will do subsequently,—but to show
the tenacity and patience of "the friend of God."

His faith, thus sorely tried by God's long delay,
is rewarded, not with an external fulfilment of the
promise, but with larger hopes, wider range of vision,
greater strength to endure, more vivid realisation of
the unseen.   "He looked for the city which hath the
foundations, whose Architect and Maker is God." *   In
the promise not a word is said about a city.   Apparently
he was still to be a nomad chief of a large and wealthy
tribe.   When God deferred again and again the fulfilment of His promise to give him "this land," His trusting servant bethought him what the delay could mean.
This was his hill of difficulty, where the two ways
part.   The worldly wisdom of unbelief would argue
from God's tardiness that the reality, when it comes,
will fall far short of the promise.   Faith, with higher
wisdom, makes sure that the delay has a purpose.

* Chap. xi. 10.

God intends to give more and better things than He promised, and is making room in the believer's heart for the greater blessings. Abraham cast about to imagine the better things. He invented a blessing, and, so to speak, inserted it for himself in the promise.

This new blessing has an earthly and a heavenly meaning. On its earthly side it represents the transition from a nomadic life to a fixed abode. Faith bridged the gulf that separates a wandering horde from the cultured greatness of civilization. The future grandeur of Zion was already held in the grasp of Abraham's faith. But the invented blessing had also a heavenly side. The more correct rendering of the Apostle's words in the Revised Version expresses this higher thought : " He looked for the city which hath the foundations "—*the* city ; for, after all, there is but one that hath the eternal foundations. It is the holy city,* the heavenly Jerusalem, seen by the faith of Abraham in the early morning of revelation, seen again in vision by the Apostle John at its close. The expression cannot mean anything that comes short of the Apostle's description of faith as the assurance of things hoped for in the unseen world. Abraham realised heaven as an eternal city, in which after death he would be gathered to his fathers. A sublime

---

* Rev. xxi. 19.

conception!—eternity not the dwelling-place of the
solitary spirit, the joy of heaven consisting in personal
fellowship for ever with the good of every age and
clime. There the past streams into the present, not,
as here, the present into the past. All are contem-
poraries there, and death is no more. Whatever makes
civilization powerful or beautiful on earth—laws, arts,
culture—all is there etherealised and endowed with
immortality. Such a city has God only for its
Architect,* God only for its Builder.† He Who conceived the plan can alone execute the design and
realise the idea.

Of this sort was Abraham's obedience. He continued to endure in the face of God's delay to fulfil the
promise. His reward consisted, not in an earthly
inheritance, not in mere salvation, but in larger hopes
and in the power of a spiritual imagination.

Second, Abraham's faith is compared with Enoch's,
whose story is most sweetly simple. He is the man
who has never doubted, across whose placid face no
dark shadow of unbelief ever sweeps. A virgin soul,
he walks with God in a time when the wickedness of
man is great in the earth and the imagination of the
thoughts of his heart is only evil continually, as Adam
walked with God in the cool of the evening before sin

---

* τεχνίτης.　　　　† δημιουργός.

had brought the hot fever of shame to his cheek.   He
walks with God, as a child with his father; "and God
takes him" into His arms.   Enoch's removal was not
like the entrance of Elijah into heaven: a victorious
conqueror returning into the city in his triumphal car.
It was the quiet passing away, without observation, of
a spirit of heaven that had sojourned for a time on
earth.   Men sought him, because they felt the loss of
his presence among them.   But they knew that God
had taken him.   They inferred his story from his
character.   In Enoch we have an instance of faith as
the faculty of realising the unseen, but not as a power
to conquer difficulties.

Compare this faith with Abraham's.   "These,"—
Abraham, Isaac, Jacob,—"all *died* in faith," or, as we
may render the word, "according to faith,"—according
to the faith which they had exhibited in their life.
Their death was after the same pattern of faith.
Enoch's contemplative life came to a fitting end in a
deathless translation to higher fellowship with God.
His way of leaving life became him.   Abraham's
repeated conflicts and victories closed with quite as
much becomingness in a last trial of his faith, when he
was called to die without having received the fulfilment
of the promises.   But he had already seen the heavenly
city and greeted it from afar.*   He saw the promises,

* ἀσπασάμενοι (xi. 13)

as the traveller beholds the gleaming mirage of the desert. The illusiveness of life is the theme of moralists when they preach resignation. It is faith only that can transform the illusions themselves into an incentive to high and holy aspirations. All profound religion is full of seeming illusions. Christ beckons us onward. When we climb this steep, His voice is heard calling to us from a higher peak. That height gained reveals a soaring mass piercing the clouds, and the voice is heard above still summoning us to fresh effort. The climber falls exhausted on the mountain-side and lays him down to die. Ever as Abraham attempted to seize the promise, it eluded his grasp. The Tantalus of heathen mythology was in Tartarus, but the Tantalus of the Bible is the man of faith, who believes the more for every failure to attain.

Such men " declare plainly that they seek a country of their own."* Let not the full force of the words escape us. The Apostle does not mean that they seek to emigrate to a new country. He has just said that they confess themselves to be " strangers and pilgrims on the earth." They are " pilgrims," because they are journeying through on their way to another country; they are " strangers," because they have come hither from another land.† His meaning is that they long to

---

* Chap. xi. 14.   † ξένοι καὶ παρεπίδημοι.

return home.   That he means this is evident from his
thinking it necessary to guard himself against the
possibility of being understood to refer to Ur of the
Chaldees.   They were not mindful of the earthly home,
the cradle of their race, which they had left for ever.
Not once did they cast a wistful look back, like Lot's
wife and the Israelites in the wilderness.   Yet they
yearned for their fatherland.*   Plato imagined that all
our knowledge is a reminiscence of what we learned
in a previous state of existence ; and Wordsworth's
exquisite lines, which cannot lose their sweet fragrance
however often they are repeated, are a reflection of the
same visionary gleam,—

> " Our birth is but a sleep and a forgetting ᵢ
> The soul that rises with us, our life's star,
>   Hath had elsewhere its setting,
>   And cometh from afar ;
>   Not in entire forgetfulness,
>   And not in utter nakedness,
> But trailing clouds of glory, do we come
>   From God, Who is our home."

Our author too suggests it; and it is true.   We
need not maintain it as an external fact in the history
of the soul, according to the old doctrine, resuscitated
in our own times, of Traducianism.   The Apostle
represents it rather as a feeling.   There is a Christian
consciousness of heaven, as if the soul had been there

---

* πατρίδα.

and longed to return.   And if it is a glorious attainment of faith to regard heaven as a city, more consol-
ing still is the hope of returning there, storm-tossed
and weather-beaten, as to a home, to look up to God
as to a Father, and to love all angels and saints as
brethren in the household of God, over which Christ is
set as a Son.   Such a hope renders feeble, sinful men
not altogether unworthy of God's Fatherhood.   For He
is not ashamed to be called their God, and Jesus Christ
is not ashamed to call them brethren.*   The proof is,
that God has prepared for them a settled abode in
the eternal city.

Third, the faith of Abraham is compared with the
faith of Abel.   In the case of Abel faith is more than
a realisation of the unseen.   For Cain also believed in
the existence of an invisible Power, and offered sacrifice.   We are expressly told in the narrative † that
" Cain brought of the fruit of the ground an offering unto
the Lord."   Yet he was a wicked man.   The Apostle
John says ‡ that " Cain was of the Evil One."   He had
the faith which St. James ascribes to the demons, who
" believe there is one God, and shudder."§   He was
possessed with the same hatred, and had also the same
faith.   It was the union of the two things in his spirit
that made him the murderer of his brother.   Our

---

* Chaps. xi. 16; ii. 11.   ‡ 1 John iii. 12.
† Gen. iv. 3.   § James ii. 19.

author points out very clearly the difference between Cain and Abel. Both sacrificed, but Abel desired righteousness. He had a conscience of sin, and sought reconciliation with God through his offering. Indeed, some of the most ancient authorities, for "God bearing witness in respect to his gifts," read "he bearing witness to God on the ground of his gifts;" that is, Abel bore witness by his sacrifice to God's righteousness and mercy. He was the first martyr, therefore, in two senses. He was God's witness, and he was slain for his righteousness. But, whether we accept this reading or the other, the Apostle presents Abel before us as the man who realised the great moral conception of righteousness. He sought, not the favours of an arbitrary Sovereign, not the mere mercy of an omnipotent Ruler, but the peace of the righteous God. It was through Abel that faith in God thus became the foundation of true ethics. He acknowledged the immutable difference between right and wrong, which is the moral theory accepted by the greater saints of the Old Testament, and in the New Testament forms the groundwork of St. Paul's forensic doctrine of the Atonement. Moreover, because Abel witnessed for righteousness by his sacrifice, his blood even cried from the ground unto God for righteous vengeance. For this is unquestionably the meaning of the words "and through his faith he being dead yet speaketh;" and

in the next chapter * the Apostle speaks of " the blood
of sprinkling, that speaketh a better thing than that
of Abel." It was the blood of one whose faith had
grasped firmly the truth of God's righteousness. His
blood, therefore, cried to the righteous God to avenge
his wrong. The Apostle speaks as if he were per-
sonifying the blood and ascribing to the slain man the
faith which he had manifested before. The action of
Abel's faith in life and, as we may safely assume, in
the very article of death, retained its power with God.
Every mouthing wound had a tongue. In like manner,
says the writer of the Epistle, the obedience of Jesus
up to and in His death made His blood efficacious for
pardon to the end of time.

But Abraham's faith excelled. Abel was prompted
to offer sacrifice by natural religiousness and an
awakened conscience ; Abraham sternly resolved to
obey a command of God. He prepared to do that
against which nature revolted, yea that which conscience forbade. Had not the story of Abel's faith
itself loudly proclaimed the sacredness of human life ?
Would not Abraham, if he offered up Isaac, become
another Cain ? Would not the dead child speak, and
his blood cry from the ground to God for vengeance ?
It was the case of a man to whom " God is greater

---

* Chap. xii. 24.

than conscience." He resolved to obey at all hazards. Hereby he assured his heart—that is, his conscience— before God in that matter wherein his heart may have condemned him.* We, it is true, in the light of a better revelation of God's character, should at once deny, without more ado, that such a command had been given by God ; and we need not fear thankfully and vehemently to declare that our absolute trust in the rightness of our own moral instincts is a higher faith than Abraham's. But he had no misgiving as to the reality of the revelation or the authority of the command. Neither do the sacred historian and the writer of the Epistle to the Hebrews question it. We also need not doubt. God met His servant at that stage of spiritual perception which he had already attained. His faith was strong in its realisation of God's authority and faithfulness. But his moral nature was not sufficiently educated to decide by the character of a command whether it was worthy of God or not. He calmly left it to Him to vindicate His own righteous- ness. Those who deny that God imposed such a hard task on Abraham must be prepared to solve still greater difficulties. For do not we also, in reference to some things, still require Abraham's faith that the Judge of all the earth will do right ? What shall we

---

* I John iii. 19, 20.

say of His permitting the terrible and universal sufferings of all living things ?   What are we to think of
the still more awful mystery of moral evil ?   Shall we
say He could not have prevented it ?   Or shall we
take refuge in the distinction between permission and
command ?   Of the two it were easier to understand
His commanding what He will not permit, as in the
sacrifice of Isaac, than to explain His permission of
what He cannot and will not command, as in the un-
doubted existence of sin.

But let us once more repeat that the greatest faith of
all is to believe, with Abel, that God is righteous, and
yet to believe, with Abraham, that God can justify His
own seeming unrighteousness, and also to believe, with
the saints of Christianity, that the test which God imposed on Abraham will nevermore be tried, because
the enlightened conscience of humanity forbids it and
invites other and more subtle tests in its place.

We must not suppose that Abraham found the command an easy one.   From the narrative in the Book
of Genesis we should infer that he expected God to
provide a substitute for Isaac : "And Abraham said,
My son, God will provide Himself a lamb for a burnt
offering; so they went both of them together."*   But
the Apostle gives us plainly to understand that Abraham

---

* Gen. xxii. 8.

offered his son because he accounted that God was able
to raise him from the dead.   Both answers are true.
They reveal to us the anxious tossings of his spirit,
seeking to account to itself for the terrible command of
Heaven.   At one moment he thinks God will not carry
matters to the bitter end.   His mind is pacified with the
thought that a substitute for Isaac will be provided.
At another moment this appeared to detract from the
awful severity of the trial, and Abraham's faith waxed
strong to obey, even though no substitute would be
found in the thicket.   Another solution would then offer
itself.   God would immediately bring Isaac back to life.
For Isaac would not cease to be, nor cease to be Isaac,
when the sacrificial knife had descended.   " God is not
God of the dead, but of the living, for all live unto
Him." *   Besides, the promise had not been with-
drawn, though it had not yet been confirmed by an
oath ; and the promise involved that the seed would be
called in Isaac, not in another son.   Both solutions were
right.   For a ram was caught in a thicket by the horns,
and Abraham did receive his son back from the dead,
not literally indeed, but in a parable.

Most expositors explain the words " in a parable "
as if they meant nothing more than " as it were," " so
to speak ; " and some have actually supposed them to

* Luke xx. 38.

refer to the birth of Isaac in his father's old age, when
Abraham was " as good as dead." *   Both interpretations do violence to the Greek expression,† which must
mean "even in a parable."   It is a brief and pregnant
allusion to *the ultimate purpose of Abraham's trial.
God intended more by it than to test faith.   The test
was meant to prepare Abraham for receiving a revelation.   On Moriah, and ever after, Isaac was more than
Isaac to Abraham.   He offered him to God as Isaac,
the son of the promise.   He received him back from
God's hand as a type of Him in Whom the promise
would be fulfilled.   Abraham had gladly received the
promise.   He now saw the day of Christ, and rejoiced.‡

---

* Chap. xi. 12   † καὶ ἐν παραβολῇ.   ‡ John viii. 56.

THE FAITH OF MOSES.

" By faith Moses, when he was born, was hid three months by his parents, because they saw he was a goodly child ; and they were not afraid of the king's commandment. By faith Moses, when he was grown up, refused to be called the son of Pharaoh's daughter ; choosing rather to be evil entreated with the people of God, than to enjoy the pleasures of sin for a season ; accounting tne reproach of Christ greater riches than the treasures of Egypt : for he looked unto the recompense of reward. By faith he forsook Egypt, not fearing the wrath of the king : for he endured, as seeing Him Who is invisible. By faith he kept the passover, and the sprinkling of the blood, that the destroyer of the first-born should not touch them."—HEB. xi. 23—28 (R. V.).

CHAPTER XII.

THE FAITH OF MOSES.

ONE difference between the Old Testament and the New is the comparative silence of the former respecting Moses and the frequent mention of him in the latter. When he has brought the children of Israel through the wilderness to the borders of the promised land, their great leader is seldom mentioned by historian, psalmist, or prophet. We might be tempted to imagine that the national life of Israel had outgrown his influence. It would without question be in a measure true. We may state the same thing on its religious side by saying that God hid the memory as well as the body of his servant, in the spirit of John Wesley's words, happily chosen for his and his brother's epitaph in Westminster Abbey, "God buries His workmen and carries on His work." But in the New Testament it is quite otherwise. No man is so frequently mentioned. Sometimes when he is not named it is easy to see that the sacred writers have him in their minds.

One reason for this remarkable difference between the two Testaments in reference to Moses is to be sought in the contrast between the earlier and later Judaism. During the ages of the old covenant Judaism was a living moral force. It gave birth to a peculiar type of heroes and saints. Speaking of Judaism in the widest possible meaning, David and Isaiah, as well as Samuel and Elijah, are its children. These men were such heroes of religion that the saints of the Christian Church have not dwarfed their greatness. But it is one of the traits of a living religion to forget the past, or rather to use it only as a stepping-stone to better things. It forgets the past in the sense in which St. Paul urges the Philippians to count what things were gain a loss, and to press on, forgetting the things which are behind, and stretching forward to the things which are before. Religion lives in its conscious, exultant power to create spiritual heroes, not in looking back to admire its own handiwork. The only religion among men that lives in its founder is Christianity. Forget Christ, and Christianity ceases to be. But the life of Mosaism was not bound up with the memory of Moses. Otherwise we may well suppose that idolatry would have crept in, even before Hezekiah found it necessary to destroy the brazen serpent.

When we come down to the times of John the Baptist and our Lord, Mosaism is to all practical ends

a dead religion.   The great movers of men's souls
came down upon the age, and were not developed out
of it.   The product of Judaism at this time was
Pharisaism, which had quite as little true faith as
Sadduceeism.   But when a religion has lost its power
to create saints, men turn their faces to the great ones
of olden times.   They raise the fallen tombstones of
the prophets, and religion is identical with hero-
worship.   An instance of this very thing may be seen
in England to-day, where Atheists have discovered
how to be devout, and Agnostics go on a pilgrimage!
"We are the disciples of Moses," cried the Pharisees.
Can any one conceive of David or Samuel calling himself a disciple of Moses ?   The notion of discipleship
to Moses does not occur in the Old Testament.   Men
never thought of such a relation.   But it is the dominant
idea of Judaism in the time of Christ.   Hence it was
brought about that he who was the servant and friend
appears in the New Testament as the antagonist.
"For the Law was given by Moses ; grace and truth
came by Jesus Christ." *   This is opposition and
rivalry.   Yet "this is that Moses which said unto the
children of Israel, A Prophet shall God raise up unto
you from among your brethren, *like unto me*." †

The notable difference between the Moses of New

---

* John i. 17.   † Acts vii. 37.

Testament times and the Moses delineated in the ancient narrative renders it especially interesting to study a passage in which the writer of the Epistle to the Hebrews takes us back to the living man, and describes the attitude of Moses himself towards Jesus Christ. Stephen told his persecutors that the founder of the Aaronic priesthood had spoken of a great Prophet to come, and Christ said that Moses wrote of Him.* But it is with joyous surprise we read in the Epistle to the Hebrews that the legislator was a believer in the same sense in which Abraham was a believer. The founder of the old covenant himself walked by faith in the new covenant.

The references to Moses made by our Lord and by Stephen sufficiently describe his mission. The special work of Moses in the history of religion was to prepare the way of the Lord Jesus Christ and make His paths straight. He was commissioned to familiarise men with the wondrous, stupendous idea of the appearing of God in human nature,—a conception almost too vast to grasp, too difficult to believe. To render it not impossible for men to accept the truth, he was instructed to create a historical type of the Incarnation. He called into being a spiritual people. He realised the magnificent idea of a Divine nation. If we may use the term, he showed to the world God appearing in the life

---

* John v. 46.

of a nation, in order to teach them the higher truth that the Word would at the remote end of the ages appear in the flesh. The nation was the Church; the Church was the State. The King would be God. The court of the King would be the temple. The ministers of the court would be the priests. The law of the State would have equal authority with the moral requirements of God's nature. For Moses apparently knew nothing of the distinction made by theologians between the civil, the ceremonial, and the moral law.

But in the passage before us we have something quite different from this. The Apostle says nothing about the creation of the covenant people out of the abject slaves of the brick-kilns. He is silent concerning the giving of the Law amid the fire and tempest of Sinai. It is plain that he wishes to tell us about the man's inner life. He represents Moses as a man of faith.

Even of his faith the apparently greatest achievements are passed over. Nothing is said of his appearances before Pharaoh; nothing of the wonderful faith that enabled him to pray with uplifted hands on the brow of the hill whilst the people were fighting God's battle in the valley; nothing of the faith with which, on the top of Pisgah, Moses died without receiving the promise. Evidently it is not the Apostle's purpose to write the panegyric of a hero.

Closer examination of the verses brings out the thought that the Apostle is tracing the growth and formation of the man's spiritual character. He means to show that faith has in it the making of a man of God. Moses became the leader of the Lord's redeemed people, the founder of the national covenant, the legislator and prophet, because he believed in God, in the future of Israel, and in the coming of the Christ. The subject of the passage is faith as the power that creates a great spiritual leader. But what is true of leaders is true also of every strong spiritual nature. No lesson can be more timely in our days. Not learning, not culture, not even genius, makes a strong doer, but faith.

The contents of the verses may be classified under four remarks :—

1. Faith gropes at first in the dark for the work of life.

2. Faith chooses the work of life.

3. Faith is a discipline of the man for the work of life.

4. Faith renders the man's life and work sacramental.

1. The initial stage in forming the servant of God is always the same,—a vague, restless, eager groping in the dark, a putting forth feelers for the light of revelation. This is often a time of childish mistakes and follies, of which he is afterwards keenly ashamed, and at which

he can sometimes afford to smile.   It often happens, **if**
the man of God is to spring from a religious family,
that his parents undergo, in a measure, this first discipline for him.   So it was in the case of Moses.   The
child was hid three months of his parents.   Why did
they hide him ?   Was it because they feared the king ?
It was because they did not fear the king.   They hid
their child by faith.   But what had faith to do with the
hiding of him ?   Had they received an announcement
from an inspired seer that their child would deliver
Israel, or that he would stand with God on the top of
Sinai and receive the Law for the people, or that he
would lead the redeemed of the Lord to the borders of
a rich land and large ?   None of these sufficient grounds
for defying the king's authority are mentioned.   The
reason given in the narrative and as well by Stephen *
and the writer of this Epistle sounds quaint, if not
childish.   They hid him because he was comely.   Yet
they hid him by faith.   The beauty of a sleeping babe
was to them a revelation, as truly a revelation as if
they had heard the voice of the angel that spoke
to Manoah or to Zacharias.   The *Scripture* narrative
contains no hint that the child's beauty was miraculous,
and, what is more to the purpose, we are not told that
God had given it as the token of His covenant.   It is an
instance of faith making a sacrament of its own, and

---

* Exod. ii. 2 ; Acts vii. 20.

seeking in what is natural its warrant for believing in the supernatural. Nothing is easier, and perhaps nothing would be more rational, than to dismiss the entire story with a contemptuous smile.

The writer of the Epistle to the Hebrews must admit that Jochebed's faith was unauthorised. But does not faith always begin in folly? Is it not at first a blind instinct, fastening on what is nearest to hand? Has not our belief in God sprung out of trust in human goodness or in nature's loveliness? To many a father has not the birth of his first-born been a revelation of Heaven? Is not such faith as Jochebed's the true explanation of the instinctive rise and wonderful vitality of infant baptism in the Christian Church? If Abraham's faith dared to look for the city which hath the foundations when God had promised only the wealth of a tented nomad, was not the mother of Moses justified, since God had given her faith, in letting the heaven-born instinct entwine with her earth-born love of her offspring? It grew with its growth, and rejoiced with its joy; but it also endured and triumphed in its sore distress, and justified its presence by saving the child. Faith is God's gift, no less than the testimony which faith accepts. Sometimes the faith is implanted when no fitting revelation is vouchsafed. But faith will live on in the darkness, until the day dawn and the day-star arise in the heart.

A wise teacher has warned us against phantom
notions and bidden us interpret rather than anticipate
nature.   But another great thinker demonstrated that
the clearest vision begins in mere groping.   Anticipa-
tions of God precede the interpretation of His message.
The immense space between instinct and genius is in
religion traversed by faith, which starts with *mera
palpatio*, but at last attains to the beatific vision of God.

2. Faith chooses the work of life.   The Apostle has
spoken of the faith that induced the parents of Moses
to hide their child three months.   Some theologians
have set much value on what they term "an implicit
faith."   The faith of Moses himself would be said by
them to be "enwrapped" in that of his parents.
Whatever we may think of this doctrine, there can
be no question that the New Testament recognises
the idea of representation.   The Church has always
upheld the unity, the solidarity, of the family.   It
sprang itself out of the family.   Perhaps its consumma-
tion on earth will be a return into the family relation.
It retains the likeness throughout its long history.   It
acknowledges that a believing husband sanctifies the
unbelieving wife, and a believing wife sanctifies the
unbelieving husband.   In like manner, a believing
parent sanctifies the children, and no one but themselves can deprive them of their privileges.   But
they can do it.   The time comes when they must

choose for themselves.   Hitherto led gently on by loving hands, they must now think and act for themselves, or be content to lose the power of independent action, and remain always children.   The risk is sometimes great.   But it cannot be evaded.   It oftentimes happens that the irrevocable step is taken unobserved by others, almost unconsciously to the man himself.   The decision has been taken in silence; the even tenor of life is not disturbed.   The world little weens that a soul has determined its own eternity in one strong resolve.

But in the case of a man destined to be a leader of his fellows, whether in thought or in action, a crisis occurs.   We use the word in its correct meaning of judgment.   It is more than a transition, more than a conversion.   He judges, and is conscious that as he judges he will be judged.   If God has any great work for the man to do, the command comes sooner or later, as if it descended audibly from heaven, that he stand alone and, in that first terrible solitariness, choose and reject.   In an educational age we may often be tempted to sneer at the doctrine of immediate conversion.   It is true, nevertheless.   A man has come to the parting of the two ways, and choice must be made, because they *are* two ways.   To no living man is it given to walk the broad and the narrow ways. Entrance is by different gates.   The history of some of the most saintly men presents an entire change of motive, of character even, and of general life, as produced through one strong act of faith.

When the Apostle wrote to the Hebrew Christians, the time was critical.   The question of Christian or not Christian brooked no delay.   The Son of man was nigh, at the doors.   Even after swift vengeance had overtaken the doomed city of Jerusalem, the urgent cry was still the same.   In the so-called "Epistle of Barnabas," in the "Pastor of Hermas," and in the priceless treasure recently brought to light, "The Teaching of the Twelve Apostles," the two ways are described: the way of life and the way of death.   Those who professed and called themselves Christians were warned to make the right choice.   It was no time for facing both ways, and halting between two opinions.

Moses too refused and chose.   This is the second scene in the history of the man.   Standing as he did at the fountain-head of nationalism, the prominence assigned to his act of individual choice and rejection is very significant.   Before his days the heirs of the promise were in the bond of God's covenant in virtue of their birth.   They were members of the elect family. After the days of Moses every Israelite enjoyed the privileges of the covenant by right of national descent. They were the elect nation.   Moses stands at the turning point.   The nation now absorbs the family, which becomes henceforth part of the larger conception. In the critical moment between the two, a great personality emerges above the confusion. The patriarchal Church of the family comes to a dispensational end in giving birth to a great man. That man's personal act of refusing the broad and choosing the narrow way marks the birth of the theocratic Church of nationalism. Before and after, personality is of secondary importance. In Moses for a moment it is everything.

Do we seek the motives that determined his choice? The Apostle mentions two, and they are really two sides of the same conception.

First, he chose to be evil-entreated with the people of God. The work of his life was to create a spiritual nation. This idea had already been presented to his mind before he refused to be called the son of Pharaoh's daughter. "He was instructed in all the wisdom of the Egyptians; and he was mighty in his words and works." * But an idea had taken possession of him. That idea had already invested the miserable and despised bondsmen with glory. Truly no man will achieve great things who does not pay homage to an idea, and is not ready to sacrifice wealth and position for the sake of what is as yet only a thought. He who sells the world for an idea is not far from the kingdom

---

* Acts vii. 22.

of heaven.   He will be prepared to forfeit all that the
world can give him for the sake of Him in Whom truth
eternally dwells in fulness and perfection.   Such a man
was Moses.   Had not his parents often told him, when
his mother was nourishing the child for Pharaoh's
daughter, of the wonderful story of their hiding him by
faith and afterwards putting him in an ark of bulrushes
by the river's brim ?   Did not his mother bring him up
to be at once the son of Pharaoh's daughter and the
deliverer of Israel ?   Was the boy not living a double
life ?   He was gradually coming to understand that he
was to be the heir of the throne, and that he would or
might be the destroyer of that throne.   May we not,
with profoundest reverence, liken it to the twofold inner
life of the Child Jesus when at Nazareth He came to
know that He, the Child of Mary, was the Son of the
Highest ?

Stephen continues the story : " When he was well-
nigh forty years old, it came into his heart to visit his
brethren the children of Israel."   " He went out unto
his brethren," we are told in the narrative, " and looked
on their burdens." *   But the author of the Epistle to
the Hebrews perceives in the act of Moses more than
love of kindred.   The slaves of Pharaoh were, in the
eyes of Moses, the people of God.   The national

---

* Exod. ii. 11.

consecration had already taken place ; he himself was already swayed by the glorious hope of delivering his brethren, the covenant people of God, from the hands of their oppressors.   This is the explanation which Stephen gives of his conduct in slaying the Egyptian. When he saw one of the children of Israel suffer wrong, he defended him and smote the Egyptian, supposing that his brethren understood how that God by his hand was giving them deliverance.   The deed was, in fact, intended to be a call to united effort.   He was throwing the gauntlet.   He was deliberately making it impossible for him to return to the former life of pomp and courtly worship.   He wished the Hebrews to understand his decision, and accept at once his leadership.   " But they understood not."

Our author pierces still deeper into the motives that swayed his spirit.   It was not a selfish ambition, nor merely a patriotic desire to put himself at the head of a host of slaves bent on asserting their rights. Simultaneous with the social movement there was a spiritual work accomplished in the personal, inner life of Moses himself.   All true, heaven-inspired revolutions in society are accompanied by a personal discipline and trial of the leaders.   This is the infallible test of the movement itself.   If the men who control it do not become themselves more profound, more pure, more spiritual, they are counterfeit leaders, and the movement they advocate is not of God. The writer of the Epistle argues from the decision of Moses to deliver his brethren that his own spiritual life was become deeper and holier. When he refused to be called the son of Pharaoh's daughter, he also rejected the pleasures of sin. He took his stand resolutely on the side of goodness. The example of Joseph was before him, of whom the same words are said : " he refused" to sin against God.

As the crisis in his own spiritual life fitted him to be the leader of a great national movement, so also his conception of that movement became a help to him to overcome the sinful temptations of Egypt. He saw that the pleasures of sin were but for a season. It is easy to supply the other side of this thought. The joy of delivering his brethren would never pass away. He welcomed the undying joy of self-sacrifice, and repudiated the momentary pleasures of self-gratification.

Second, he accounted the reproach of Christ greater riches than the treasures of Egypt. Not only the people of God, but also the Christ of God, determined his choice. An idea is not enough. It must rest on a person, and that person must be greater than the idea. He may be himself but an idea. But, even when it is so, he is the glorious thought in which all the other hopes and imaginations of faith centre and merge. If he is more than an idea, if it is a living person that controls the man's thoughts and becomes the motive of his life, a new quality will then enter into that life. Conscience will awake. The question of doing what is right will control ambition, if it will not quite absorb it. Treachery to the idea of life will now be felt to be a sin, if conscience has pronounced that the idea itself is not immoral, but good and noble. For, when conscience permits, faith will not lag behind, and will proclaim that the moral is also spiritual, that the spiritual is an ever-abiding possession.

Many expositors strive hard to make the words mean something else than the reproach which Christ Himself suffered. It is marvellous that the great doctrine of Christ's personal activity in the Church before His incarnation should have so entirely escaped the notice of the older school of English theology. On this passage, for instance, such commentators as Macknight, Whitby, Scott, explain the words to mean that Moses esteemed the scoffs cast on the Israelites for expecting the Christ to arise from among them greater riches than the treasures of Egypt. The more profound exegesis of Germany has made the truth of Christ's pre-existence essential to the theology of the New Testament. Far from being an innovation, it has brought us back to the view of the greater theologians in every age of the Church.

We cannot enter into the general question. Con-

fining ourselves to the subject in hand, the faith of
Moses, why may we not suppose that he had heard
of the patriarch Jacob's blessing on Judah? It had
been uttered in the land of Egypt, where Moses was
brought up. It spoke of a Lawgiver. Did not the
consciousness of his own mission lead Moses to apply
the reference to the long succession of leaders, whether
judges or kings or prophets, who would follow in his
wake? If so, could he have altogether misunderstood
the promise of the Shiloh? Jacob had spoken of a
personal King, Whom the people would obey. But
nowhere in the Old Testament, not once in the history
of Moses, is the coming of Messiah represented as the
goal of the national development. Christ is not the
flowering of Judaism. On the contrary, the Angel
of the covenant established through Moses is not
a ministering servant, sent forth to minister on the
chosen people. He is the Lord Jehovah Himself.
Christ was with Israel, and Moses knew it. We may
admit the vagueness of his conception, but we cannot
deny the conception. To Moses, as to the Psalmist,
the reproaches of them that reproached Israel fell on
the Christ. Community in suffering was enough to
ensure community in the glory to be revealed. Suffering with Christ, they would also be glorified with
Christ. This was the recompense of reward to which
Moses looked.

The lesson taught to the Hebrew Christians by the decision of Moses is loyalty to truth and loyalty to Jesus Christ.

3. Faith is a discipline for the work of life. Moses has made his final choice. Conscience is thoroughly awake, and eager aspirations fill his soul. But he is not yet strong. Men of large ideas are often found to be lacking in courage. A cloistered is often a fugitive virtue. But, apart from want of practical resolution to face the difficulties of the situation, special training is needed for special work. Israel had come into Egypt to endure chastening and be made fit for national independence. But in Egypt Moses was a courtier, perhaps heir to the throne. That he may be chastened and fitted for his share of the work which God was about to accomplish towards His people, he must be driven out of Egypt into the wilderness. Every servant of God is sent into the wilderness. St. Paul was three years in Arabia between his conversion and his entrance on the work of the ministry. Jesus Himself was led up of the Spirit into the wilderness. He learned endurance in forty days, Moses in forty years.

It will be seen that we accept the explanation of the twenty-seventh verse given by all expositors down to the time of De Lyra and Calvin. But in modern times it has been customary to say that the Apostle refers to the final departure of the children of Israel out of Egypt with

a strong hand and outstretched arm.   Our reasons for
preferring the other view are these.   The departure of
the Israelites through the Red Sea is mentioned subsequently ; an event that occurred before the people
left Egypt is mentioned in the next verse, and it is
very improbable that the writer would refer to their
departure first, then to the events that preceded, then
once more speak of their departure.   Further, the word
well rendered by the Old and the Revised Versions
" forsook " expresses precisely the notion of going out
alone, in despondency, as if Moses had abandoned the
hope of being the deliverer of Israel.   If we have
correctly understood the Apostle's purpose in the entire
passage, this is the very notion which we should expect
him to introduce.   Moses forsakes Egypt, deserts his
brethren, abandons his work.   He flees from the
vengeance of Pharaoh.   Yet all this fear, hopelessness,
and unbelief is only the partial aspect of what, taken
as a whole, is the action of faith.   He still believes in
his glorious idea, and is still willing to bear the reproach
of Christ.   He will not return to the court and make
his submission to the king.   But the time is not come,
he thinks, or he is not the man to deliver Israel.
Forty years afterwards he is still loath to be sent.   He
forsook Egypt because the people did not believe him ;
after forty years he asks the Lord to send another for
the very same reason : " Behold, they will not believe

me, nor hearken unto my voice." But we should be obtuse indeed if we failed to recognise the faith that underlies his despondency. Doubt is oftentimes partial faith.

Let us place ourselves in his position. He refuses the selfish luxury and worldly glory of Pharaoh's court, that he may rush to deliver his brethren. He brings with him the consciousness of superiority, and at once assumes the duty of composing their quarrels. Evidently he is a believer in God, but a believer also in himself. Such men are not God's instruments. He will have a man be the one thing or the other. If the man is self-confident, conscious of his own prowess, oblivious of God or a denier of Him, the Most High can use him to do His work, to his own destruction. If the man has no confidence in the flesh, knows his utter weak·· ness and very nothingness, and yields himself to God's hand entirely, with no by-ends to seek, him too God uses to do His work, to the man's own salvation. But Moses strove to combine faith in God and in himself. He was at once thwarted. His brethren taunted him, when he expected to be trusted and honoured. Despondency takes possession of his spirit. But his trepidation is on the surface. Beneath it is a great deep of faith. What he now needs is discipline. God leads him to the back of the wilderness. The courtier serves as a herdsman. Far removed from the monumental

literature of Egypt, he communes with himself, and
with nature's mighty visions.	He gazes upon the
dread and silent mountain, hallowed of old as the
habitation of God.	He had already, in Egypt, learned
the faith of Joseph and of Jacob.	Now, in Midian, he
will imbibe the faith of Isaac and of Abraham.	Far
from the busy haunts of men, the din of cities, the stir
of the market-place, he will learn how to pray, how to
divest himself of all confidence in the flesh, and how
to worship the Invisible alone.	For "he endured as
seeing Him Who is invisible."	Do not paraphrase it
"the invisible *King*."	That is too narrow.	It was not
Pharaoh only that had vanished out of his sight and
out of his thoughts.	Moses himself had disappeared.
He had broken down when he trusted himself.	He
now endures, because he sees nought but God.	Surely
he was in the same blessed state of mind in which St.
Paul was when he said, "I live, yet not I, but Christ
liveth in me."	When Moses and when Paul ceased
to be anything, and God was to them everything, they
were strong to endure.*

4. Faith renders the work of life sacramental.
The long period of discipline has drawn to a close.
The self-confidence of Moses has been fully subdued.

---

* After penning the above the writer of these pages saw that, in his
view of the purpose of the sojourn in Midian, he had been anticipated
by Kurtz (*History of the Old Covenant*).

" He supposed that his brethren understood how that
God by his hand was giving them deliverance."
These, says Stephen, were his thoughts before he fled
from Egypt. Very different is his language after the
probation of the wilderness : "Who am I, that I should
go unto Pharaoh, and that I should bring forth the
children of Israel out of Egypt?" Four times he
pleads and deprecates. Not until the anger of the
Lord is kindled against him does he take heart to
attempt the formidable task.

The Hebrews had been more than two hundred years
in the house of bondage. So far as we know, the
Lord had not once appeared or spoken to men for six
generations. No revelation was given between Jacob's
vision at Beersheba* and the vision of the burning
bush. We may well believe that there were in those
days mockers, saying, The age of miracles is past ;
the supernatural is played out. But Moses henceforth
lives in a veritable world of miracles. The supernatural came with a rush, like the waking of a sleeping
volcano. Signs and wonders encompass him on every
side. The bush burns unconsumed ; the rod in his
hand is cast on the ground, and becomes a serpent ; he
takes the serpent in his hand again, and it becomes a
rod ; he puts his hand into his bosom, and it is leprous ;
he puts the leprous hand into his bosom, and it is as

---

* Gen. xlvi. 2.

his other flesh. When he returns into Egypt, signs vie
with signs, God with demons. Plague follows plague.
Moses lifts up his rod over the sea, and the children of
Israel go on dry ground through the midst of the sea.
At last he stands once more on Horeb. But in the
short interval between the day when one poor thorn-
bush of the desert glowed with flame and the day on
which Sinai was altogether on a smoke and the whole
mountain quaked, a religious revolution had occurred
second only to one in the history of the race. At
the touch of their leader's wand a nation was born in
a day. The immense transition from the Church in a
family to a holy nation was brought about suddenly,
but effectively, when the people were hopeless outcasts
and Moses himself had lost heart.

Such a revolution must be inaugurated with sacrifice
and with sacrament. The sins of the past must be
expiated and forgiven, and the people, cleansed from
the guilt of their too frequent apostasy from the God
of their fathers, must be dedicated anew to the service
of Jehovah. The patriarchal dispensation expired in
the birth of a holy nation. The Passover was both a
sacrifice and a sacrament, an expiation and a consecration. It retained its sacrificial character till Christ, the
true Paschal Lamb, was slain. As a sacrifice it then
ceased. But sacrament continues, and will continue as
long as the Church exists on earth.

Moses had seen the invisible God. The burning bush had symbolized the sacramental nature of the work which he had been called to do. God would be in Israel as He was in the bush, and Israel would not be consumed. He Who is to His foes a consuming fire dwells among His people, as the vital heat and glow of their national life. The eye that can see Him is faith. This is the power that can transform the whole life of man, and make it sacramental. Too long has man's earthly existence been divided into two separate spheres. On the one side and for a stated time he lives to God ; on the other side he relinquishes himself for a period to the pursuits of the world. We seem to think that the secular cannot be religious, and, consequently, that the religiousness of one day or of one place will make amends for the irreligion of the rest of life. The Passover consecrated a nation. Baptism and the Lord's Supper have, times without number, consecrated the individual. The true Christian life draws its vital sap from God. It is not cleverness and worldly success, but unselfish loyalty to the supernatural, and incessant prayer, that marks the man who lives by faith.

A CLOUD OF WITNESSES.

"By faith Isaac blessed Jacob and Esau, even concerning things to come. By faith Jacob, when he was a-dying, blessed each of the sons of Joseph ; and worshipped, *leaning* upon the top of his staff. By faith Joseph, when his end was nigh, made mention of the departure of the children of Israel ; and gave commandment concerning his bones. . . . By faith the walls of Jericho fell down, after they had been compassed about for seven days. By faith Rahab the harlot perished not with them that were disobedient, having received the spies with peace. And what shall I more say ? for the time will fail me if I tell of Gideon, Barak, Samson, Jephthah ; of David and Samuel and the prophets : who through faith subdued kingdoms, wrought righteousness, obtained promises, stopped the mouths of lions, quenched the power of fire, escaped the edge of the sword, from weakness were made strong, waxed mighty in war, turned to flight armies of aliens. Women received their dead by a resurrection : and others were tortured, not accepting their deliverance ; that they might obtain a better resurrection : and others had trial of mockings and scourgings, yea, moreover of bonds and imprisonment : they were stoned, they were sawn asunder, they were tempted, they were slain with the sword : they went about in sheepskins, in goatskins ; being destitute, afflicted, evil-entreated (of whom the world was not worthy), wandering in deserts and mountains and caves, and the holes of the earth. And these all, having had witness borne to them through their faith, received not the promise, God having provided some better thing concerning us, that apart from us they should not be made perfect. Therefore let us also, seeing we are compassed about with so great a cloud of witnesses, lay aside every weight, and the sin which doth so easily beset us, and let us run with patience the race that is set before us."—HEB. xi. 20—xii. 1 (R.V.).

CHAPTER XIII.

A CLOUD OF WITNESSES.

TIME fails us to dilate on the faith of the other saints of the old covenant. But they must not be passed over in silence. The impression produced by our author's splendid roll of the heroes of faith in the eleventh chapter is the result quite as much of an accumulation of examples as of the special greatness of a few among them. At the close they appear like an overhanging " cloud " of witnesses for God.

By faith Isaac blessed Jacob and Esau ; and Jacob, dying in a strange land, blessed the sons of Joseph, distinguishing wittingly, and bestowing on *each* * his own peculiar blessing. His faith became a prophetic inspiration, and even distinguished between the future of Ephraim and the future of Manasseh. He did not create the blessing. He was only a steward of God's mysteries. Faith well understood its own limitations. But it drew its inspiration to foretell what was to come from a remembrance of God's faithfulness in the past.

---

* ἕκαστον (xi. 21).

For, before* he gave his blessing, he had bowed his head in worship, leaning upon the top of his staff. In his dying hour he recalled the day on which he had passed over Jordan with his staff,—a day remembered by him once before, when he had become two bands, wrestled with the angel, and halted on his thigh. His staff had become his token of the covenant, his reminder of God's faithfulness, his sacrament, or visible sign of an invisible grace.

Joseph, though he was so completely Egyptianised that he did not, like Jacob, ask to be buried in Canaan, and only two of his sons became, through Jacob's blessing, heirs of the promise, yet gave commandment concerning his bones. His faith believed that the promise given to Abraham would be fulfilled. The children of Israel might dwell in Goshen and prosper. But they would sooner or later return to Canaan. When his end drew near, his Egyptian greatness was forgotten. The piety of his childhood returned. He remembered God's promise to his fathers. Perhaps it was his father Jacob's dying blessing that had revived the thoughts of the past and fanned his faith into a steady flame.

" By faith the walls of Jericho fell down." † When the Israelites had crossed Jordan and eaten of the old

---

* Gen. xlvii. 31.   † Chap. xi. 30.

corn of the land, the manna ceased. The period of continued miracle came to an end. Henceforth they would smite their enemies with their armed thousands. But one signal miracle the Lord would yet perform in the sight of all Israel. The walls of the first city they came to would fall down flat, when the seven priests would blow with the trumpets of rams' horns the seventh time on the seventh day. Israel believed, and as God had said, so it came to pass.

The treachery of a harlot even is mentioned by the Apostle as an instance of faith.* Justly. For, whilst her past life and present act were neither better nor worse than the morality of her time, she saw the hand of the God of heaven in the conquest of the land, and bowed to His decision. This was a greater faith than that of her daughter-in-law, Ruth, whose name is not mentioned. Ruth believed in Naomi and, as a consequence, accepted Naomi's God and. people. † Rahab believed in God first, and, therefore, accepted the Israelitish conquest and adopted the nationality of the conquerors. ‡

Of the judges the Apostle selects four : Gideon, Barak, Samson, Jephthah. The mention of Barak must be understood to include Deborah, who was the mind and heart that moved Barak's arm ; and Deborah

---

* Chap. xi. 31.　† Ruth i. 16.　‡ Matt. i. 5.

was a prophetess of the Lord. She and Barak wrought their mighty deeds and sang their pæan in faith.* Gideon put the Midianites to flight by faith; for he knew that his sword was the sword of the Lord. † Jephthah was a man of faith; for he vowed a vow unto the Lord, and would not go back. ‡ Samson had faith; for he was a Nazarite to God from his mother's womb, and in his last extremity called unto the Lord and prayed. §

The Apostle does not name Othniel, Ehud, Shamgar, and the rest. The Spirit of the Lord came upon them also. They too were mighty through God. But the narrative does not tell us that they prayed, or that their soul consciously and believingly responded to the voice of Heaven. Alaric, while on his march towards Rome, said to a holy monk, who entreated him to spare the city, that he did not go of his own will, but that One was continually urging him forward to take it.‖ Many are the scourges of God that know not the hand that wields them.

Individuals " through faith subdued kingdoms."¶

---

* Judges iv. and v.
† Judges vii. 18.
‡ Judges xi. 35.
§ Judges xiii. 7 ; xvi. 28.
‖ Robertson, *History of the Christian Church,* book ii., chap. vii.
¶ Chap. xi. 33.

Gideon dispersed the Midianites;* Barak discomfited
Sisera, the captain of Jabin king of Canaan's host;
Jephthah smote the Ammonites;† David held the
Philistines in check,‡ measured Moab with a line, §
and put garrisons in Syria of Damascus. Samuel
" wrought righteousness," and taught the people the
good and the right way.‖ David " obtained the fulfilment of God's promises :" his house was blessed that
it should continue for ever before God.¶ Daniel's faith
stopped the mouths of lions.** The faith of Shadrach,
Meshach, and Abednego trusted in God, and quenched
the power of the fire, without extinguishing its flame.††
Elijah escaped the edge of Ahab's sword. ‡‡ Elisha's
faith saw the mountain full of horses and chariots of
fire round about him. §§ Hezekiah " from weakness
was made strong." ‖‖ The Maccabæan princes waxed
mighty in war and turned to flight armies of aliens.¶¶
The widow of Zarephath*** and the Shunammite††† received their dead back into their embrace in consequence
of ‡‡‡ a resurrection wrought by the faith of the prophets. Others refused deliverance, gladly accepting
the alternative to unfaithfulness, to be beaten to death,

---

* Judges vii.
† Judges xi. 33.
‡ 2 Sam. v. 25.
§ 2 Sam. viii. 2, 6.
‖ 1 Sam. xii. 23.

¶ 2 Sam. vii. 28, 29.
** Dan. vi. 22.
†† Dan. iii. 27, 28.
‡‡ 1 Kings xix. 1—3.
§§ 2 Kings vi. 17.

‖‖ 2 Kings xx. 5.
¶¶ 1 Macc. v.
*** 1 Kings xvii. 22.
††† 2 Kings iv. 35.
‡‡‡ ἐξ (chap. xi. 35).

that they might be accounted worthy * to attain the better world and the resurrection, not *of*, but *from*, the dead, which is the resurrection to eternal life. Such a man was the aged Eleazar in the time of the Maccabees.†

Zechariah was stoned to death at the commandment of Joash the king in the court of the house of the Lord.‡ Isaiah is said to have been sawn asunder in extreme old age by the order of Manasseh. Others were burnt § by Antiochus Epiphanes. Elijah had no settled abode, but went from place to place clad in a garment of hair, the skin of sheep or goat. It ought not to be a matter of surprise that these men of God had no dwelling-place, but were, like the Apostles after them, buffeted, persecuted, defamed, and made as the filth of the world, the offscouring of all things. For the world was not worthy of them. The world crucified their Lord, and they would be ashamed of accepting better treatment than He received. By the world is meant the life of those who know not Christ. The men of faith were driven out of the cities into the desert, out of homes into prisons. But their faith was an assurance of things hoped for and, therefore, a solvent of fear. Their proving of things not seen rendered the prison, as Tertullian says,‖ a place of retirement, and the

---

* Luke xx. 35. ‡ 2 Chron. xxiv. 21.
† 2 Macc· vi. 19. § Reading ἐπρήσθησαν.

Ad Martyras, 2.

desert a welcome escape from the abominations that met their eyes wherever the world had set up its vanity fair.

All these sturdy men of faith have had witness borne to them in Scripture. This honour they won from time to time, as the Spirit of Christ, which was in the prophets, saw fit to encourage the people of God on earth by their example. Are we forbidden to suppose that this witness to their faith gladdened their own glorified spirits, and calmed their eager expectation of the day when the promise would be fulfilled? For, after all, their reward was not the testimony of Scripture, but their own perfection. Now this perfection is described throughout the Epistle as a priestly consecration. It expresses fitness for entering into immediate communion with God. This was the final fulfilment of the promise. This was the blessing which the saints under the old covenant had not obtained. The way of the holiest had not yet been opened.* Consequently their faith consisted essentially in endurance. "None of these received the promise," but patiently waited. This is inferred concerning them from the testimony of Scripture that they believed. Their faith must have manifested itself in this form,—endurance. To us, at length, the promise has been fulfilled. God has spoken

---

* Chap. ix. 8.

unto us in His Son.   We have a great High-priest, Who
has passed through the heavens.   The Son, as High-
priest, has been perfected for evermore ; that is, He is
endowed with fitness to enter into the true holiest
place.   He has perfected also for ever them that are
sanctified : freed from guilt as worshippers, they enter
the holiest through a priestly consecration.   The new
and living way has been dedicated through the veil.

But the important point is that the fulfilment of the
promise has not dispensed with the necessity for faith.
We saw, in an earlier chapter, that the revelation of
the Sabbath advances from lower forms of rest to
higher and more spiritual.   The more stubborn the
unbelief of men became, the more fully the revelation
of God's promise opened up.   The thought is somewhat similar in the present passage.   The final form
which God's promise assumes is an advance on any
fulfilment vouchsafed to the saints of the old covenant
during their earthly life.   It now includes perfection,
or fitness to enter into the holiest through the blood
of Christ.   It means immediate communion with God.
Far from dispensing with faith, this form of the
promise demands the exercise of a still better faith
than the fathers had.   They endured by faith ; we
through faith enter the holiest.   To them, as well as
to us, faith is an assurance of things hoped for and a
proving of things not seen ; but our assurance must

incite us to draw near with boldness unto the throne
of grace, to draw near with a true heart in *full assurance* of faith.   This is the better faith which is not
once ascribed in the eleventh chapter to the saints of
the Old Testament.   On the contrary, we are given to
understand * that they, through fear of death, were all
their lifetime subject to bondage.   But Christ has
abolished death.   For we enter into the presence of
God, not through death, but through faith.

In accordance with this, the Apostle says that
"God provided some better thing concerning us." †
These words cannot mean that God provided some
better thing *for* us than He had provided for the
fathers.   Such a notion would not be true.   The
promise was made to Abraham, and is now fulfilled
to all the heirs alike; that is, to those who are of the
faith of Abraham.   The author says "concerning," ‡
not "for."   The idea is that God foresaw we would,
and provided (for the word implies both things) that
we should, manifest a better kind of faith than it was
possible for the fathers to show, better in so far
as power to enter the holiest place is better than
endurance.

But the author adds another thought.   Through
the exercise of the better faith by us, the fathers also

---

* Chap. ii. 15.   † Chap. xi. 40.   ‡ περί.

enter with us into the holiest place. "Apart from us they could not be made perfect." The priestly consecration becomes theirs through us. Such is the unity of the Church, and such the power of faith, that those who could not believe, or could not believe in a certain way, for themselves, receive the fulness of the blessing through the faith of others. Nothing less will do justice to the Apostle's words than the notion that the saints of the old covenant have, through the faith of the Christian Church, entered into more immediate and intimate communion with God than they had before, though in heaven.

We now understand why they take so deep an interest in the running of the Christian athletes on earth. They surround their course, like a great cloud. They know that they will enter into the holiest if we win the race. For every new victory of faith on earth, there is a new revelation of God in heaven. Even the angels, the principalities and powers in the heavenly places, learn, says St. Paul, through the Church the manifold wisdom of God.* How much more will the saints, members of the Church, brethren of Christ, be better able to apprehend the love and power of God, Who makes weak, sinful men conquerors over death and its fear.

* Eph. iii. 10.

The word "witnesses"* does not itself refer to
their looking on, as spectators of the race.   Another
word would almost certainly have been used to express
this notion, which is moreover contained in the phrase
"having so great a cloud surrounding † us."   The
thought seems to be that the men to whose faith the
Spirit of Christ in Scripture bare witness were themselves witnesses for God in a godless world, in the same
sense in which Christ tells His disciples that they
were His witnesses, and Ananias tells Saul that he
would be a witness for Christ. ‡   Every one who
confessed Christ before men, him did Christ also
confess before His Church which is on earth, and
does now confess before His Father in heaven, by
leading him into God's immediate presence.

---

* μαρτύρων (xii. 1).   † περικείμενον.   ‡ Acts i. 8 ; xxii. 14.

CONFLICT.

"Therefore let us also, seeing we are compassed about with so great a cloud of witnesses, lay aside every weight, and the sin which doth so easily beset us, and let us run with patience the race that is set before us, looking unto Jesus the Author and Perfecter of *our* faith, who for the joy that was set before Him endured the Cross, despising shame, and hath sat down at the right hand of the throne of God. For consider Him that hath endured such gainsaying of sinners against themselves, that ye wax not weary, fainting in your souls. Ye have not yet resisted unto blood, striving against sin : and ye have forgotten the exhortation, which reasoneth with you as with sons,

> My son, regard not lightly the chastening of the Lord,
> Nor faint when thou art reproved of Him ;
> For whom the Lord loveth He chasteneth,
> And scourgeth every son whom He receiveth.

It is for chastening that ye endure ; God dealeth with you as with sons ; for what son is there whom *his* father chasteneth not ? But if ye are without chastening, whereof all have been made partakers, then are ye bastards, and not sons. Furthermore, we had the fathers of our flesh to chasten us, and we gave them reverence : shall we not much rather be in subjection unto the Father of spirits, and live ? For they verily for a few days chastened *us* as seemed good to them ; but He for *our* profit, that *we* may be partakers of His holiness. All chastening seemeth for the present to be not joyous, but grievous : yet afterward it yieldeth peaceable fruit unto them that have been exercised thereby, *even the fruit* of righteousness. Wherefore lift up the hands that hang down, and the palsied knees ; and make straight paths for your feet, that that which is lame be not turned out of the way, but rather be healed. Follow after peace with all men, and the sanctification without which no man shall see the Lord : looking carefully lest *there be* any man that falleth short of the grace of God ; lest any root of bitterness springing up trouble *you*, and thereby the many be defiled ; lest *there be* any fornicator, or profane person, as Esau, who for one mess of meat sold his own birthright. For ye know that even when he afterward desired to inherit the blessing, he was rejected (for he found no place of repent-ance), though he sought it diligently with tears."—HEB. xii. 1—17 (R.V.).

CHAPTER XIV.

CONFLICT.

THE author has told his readers that they have need of endurance; * but when he connects this endurance with faith, he describes faith, not as an enduring of present evils, but as an assurance of things hoped for in the future. His meaning undoubtedly is that assurance of the future gives strength to endure the present. These are two distinct aspects of faith. In the eleventh chapter both sides of faith are illustrated in the long catalogue of believers under the Old Testament. Examples of men waiting for the promise and having an assurance of things hoped for come first. They are Abel, Enoch, Noah, Abraham, Isaac, Jacob, and Joseph. In some measure these witnesses of God suffered; but the more prominent feature of their faith was expectation of a future blessing. Moses is next mentioned. He marks a transition. In him the two qualities of faith appear to strive for the pre-eminence. He chooses to be evil entreated with the

---

* ὑπομονή (x. 36).

people of God, because he knows that the enjoyment of sin is short-lived; he suffers the reproach of Christ, and looks away from it to the recompense of reward. After him conflict and endurance are more prominent in the history of believers than assurance of the future. Many of these later heroes of faith had a more or less dim vision of the unseen; and in the case of those of whose faith nothing is said in the Old Testament except that they endured, the other phase of this spiritual power is not wanting. For the Church is one through the ages, and the clear eye of an earlier period cannot be disconnected from the strong arm of a later time.

In the twelfth chapter the two aspects of faith exemplified in the saints of the Old Testament are urged on the Hebrew Christians. Now practically for the first time in the Epistle the writer addresses himself to the difficulties and discouragements of a state of conflict. In the earlier chapters he exhorted his readers to hold fast their own individual confession of Christ. In the later portions he exhorted them to quicken the faith of their brethren in the Church assemblies. But his account of the worthies of the Old Testament in the previous chapter has revealed a special adaptedness in faith to meet the actual condition of his readers. We gather from the tenor of the passage that the Church had to contend against evil men. Who they

were we do not know. They were "the sinners."
Our author is claiming for the Christian Church the
right to speak of the men outside in the language used
by Jews concerning the heathen ; and it is not at all
unlikely that the unbelieving Jews themselves are here
meant.   His readers had to endure the gainsaying of
sinners, who poured contempt on Christianity, as they
had also covered Christ Himself with shame.   The
Church might have to resist unto blood in striving
against the encompassing sin.   Peace is to be sought
and followed after with all men, but not to the injury
of that sanctification without which no man shall see
the Lord.*   The true people of God must go forth
unto Jesus without the camp of Judaism, bearing His
reproach.†

This is an advance in the thought.   Our author does
not exhort his readers individually to steadfastness,
nor the Church collectively to mutual oversight.   He
has before his eyes the conflict of the Church against
wicked men, whether in sheep's clothing or without the
fold.   The purport of the passage may be thus stated :
Faith as a hope of the future is a faith to endure in
the present conflict against men.   The reverse of this
is equally true and important : that faith as a strength
to endure the gainsaying of men is the faith that

---

* Chap. xii 14.   † Chap. xiii. 13.

presses on toward the goal unto the prize of the high calling of God in Christ Jesus.

The connecting link between these two representations of faith is to be found in the illustration with which the chapter opens. A race implies both a hope and a contest.

The hope of faith is simple and well understood. It has been made abundantly clear in the Epistle. It is to obtain the fulfilment of the promise made to Abraham and renewed to other believers time after time under the old covenant. "For we who believe do enter into God's rest."* "They that have been called receive the promise of the eternal inheritance."† "We have boldness to enter into the holiest by the blood of Jesus."‡ In the latter part of the chapter the writer speaks of his readers as having already attained. They have come to God, and to the spirits of just men made perfect, and to Jesus, the Mediator of the new covenant. In the first verse he urges them to run the race, so as to secure for themselves the blessing. He points them to Jesus, Who has run the race before them and won the crown, Who sits on the right hand of God, with authority to reward all who reach the goal. Both representations are perfectly consistent. Men do enter into immediate communion with God on earth; but they attain it by effort of faith.

---

* Chap. iv. 3.   † Chap. ix. 15.   ‡ Chap. x. 19.

Such is the aim of faith. The conflict is more complex and difficult to explain. There is, first of all, a conflict in the preparatory training, and this is twofold. We have to strive against ourselves and against the world. We must put away our own grossness,* as athletes rid themselves by severe training of all superfluous flesh. Then we must also put away from us the sin that surrounds us, that quite besets us, on all sides,† whether in the world or in the Church, as runners must have the course cleared and the crowd of onlookers that press around removed far enough to give them the sense of breathing freely and running unimpeded in a large space. The word "besetting" does not refer to the special sin to which every individual is most prone. No thoughtful man but has felt himself encompassed by sin, not merely as a temptation, but much more as an overpowering force, silent, passive, closing in upon him on all sides,— a constant pressure from which there is no escape. The sin and misery of the world has staggered reason and left men utterly powerless to resist or to alleviate the infinite evil. Faith alone surmounts these preliminary difficulties of the Christian life. Faith delivers us from grossness of spirit, from lethargy, earthliness, stupor. Faith will also lift us above the terrible

---

* ὄγκον (xii. 1).   † εὐπερίστατον.

pressure of the world's sin. Faith has the heart that still hopes, and the hand that still saves. Faith resolutely puts away from her whatever threatens to overwhelm and impede, and makes for herself a large room to move freely in.

Then comes the actual contest. Our author says "contest." * For the conflict is against evil men. Yet it is, in a true and vital sense, not a contest of the kind which the word naturally suggests. Here the effort is not to be first at the goal. We run the race "through endurance." Mental suffering is of the essence of the conflict. Our success in winning the prize does not mean the failure of others. The failure of our rivals does not imply that we attain the mark. In fact, the Christian life is not the competition of rivals, but the enduring of shame at the hands of evil men, which endurance is a discipline. Maybe we do not sufficiently lay to heart that the discipline of life consists mainly in overcoming rightly and well the antagonism of men. The one bitterness in the life of our Lord Himself was the malice of the wicked. Apart from that unrelenting hatred we may regard His short life as serenely happy. The warning which He addressed to His disciples was that they should beware of men. But, though wisdom is necessary, the

* ἀγῶνα.

conflict must not be shunned. When it is over, nothing will more astonish the man of faith than that he should have been afraid, so weak did malice prove to be.

To run our course successfully, we must keep our eyes steadily fixed on Jesus.* It is true we are compassed about with a cloud of God's faithful witnesses. But they are a cloud. The word signifies not merely that they are a large multitude, but also that we cannot distinguish individuals in the immense gathering of those who have gone before. The Church has always cherished a hope that the saints of heaven are near us, perhaps seeing our efforts to follow their glorious example. Beyond this we dare not go. Personal communion is possible to the believer on earth with One only of the inhabitants of the spiritual world. That One is Jesus Christ. Even faith cannot discern the individual saints that compose the cloud. But it can look away from all of them to Jesus. It looks unto Jesus as He is and as He was: as He is for help; as He was for a perfect example.

1. Faith regards Jesus as He is,—the "Leader and Perfecter." The words are an allusion to what the writer has already told us in the Epistle concerning Jesus. He is "the Captain or Leader of our salvation,"†

---

* Chap. xii. 2.   † ἀρχηγόν (ii. 10).

and " by one offering He hath perfected for ever them that are sanctified." * He leads onward our faith till we attain the goal, and for every advance we make in the course He strengthens, sustains, and in the end completes our faith. The runner, when he seizes the crown, will not be found to have been exhausted by his efforts. High attainments demand a correspondingly great faith.

Many expositors think the words which we have rendered " Leader " and " Perfecter " refer to Christ's own faith. But the words will hardly admit of this meaning. Others think they are intended to convey the notion that Christ is the Author of our faith in its weak beginnings and the Finisher of it when it attains perfection. But the use which the Apostle has made of the words " Leader of salvation " in chap. ii. seems to prove that here also he understands by " Leader " One Who will bring our faith onward safely to the end of the course. The distinction is rather between rendering us certain of winning the crown and making our faith large and noble enough to be worthy of wearing it.

2. Faith regards Jesus as He was on earth, the perfect example of victory through endurance. He has acquired His power .to lead onward and to make

---

* τετελείωκεν (x. 14).

perfect our faith by His own exercise of faith. He is "Leader" because He is "Forerunner;" * He is "Perfecter" because He Himself has been perfected.† He endured a cross. The author leaves it to his readers to imagine all that is implied in the awful word. More is involved in the Cross than shame. For the shame of the Cross He could afford to despise. But there was in the Cross what He did not despise; yea, what drew tears and strong cries from Him in the agony of His soul. Concerning *this*, whatever it was, the author is here silent, because it was peculiar to Christ, and could never become an example to others, except indeed in the faith that enabled Him to endure it.

Even in the gainsaying of men there was an element which He did not despise, but endured. He understood that their gainsaying was against themselves.‡ It would end, not merely in putting Him to an open shame, but in their own destruction. This caused keen suffering to His holy and loving spirit. But He endured it, as He endured the Cross itself in all its mysterious import. He did not permit the sin and perdition of the world to overwhelm Him. His faith resolutely put away from Him the deadly pressure. On the one hand, He did not despise sin; on the other, He was not crushed by its weight. He calmly endured.

---

* πρόδρομος (vi. 20).   † τετελειωμένον (vii. 28).
‡ Reading εἰς ἑαυτούς (xii. 3).

But He endured through faith, as an assurance of things hoped for and the proving of things not seen. He hoped to attain the joy which was set before Him as the prize to be won.   The connection of the thought with the general subject of the whole passage satisfies us that the words translated "for the joy set before Him" are correctly so rendered, and do not mean that Christ chose the suffering and shame of the Cross in preference to the enjoyment of sin   This also is perfectly true, and more true of Christ than it was even of Moses.   But the Apostle's main idea throughout is that faith in the form of assurance and faith in the form of enduring go together.   Jesus endured because He looked for a future joy as His recompense of reward ; He attained the joy through His endurance.

But, as more than shame was involved in His Cross, more also than joy was reserved for Him in reward. Through His Cross He became "the Leader and Perfecter" of our faith.   He was exalted to be the Sanctifier of His people.   "He has sat down on the right hand of God."

Our author proceeds : Weigh this in the balance.* Compare this quality of faith with your own.   Consider who He was and what you are.   When you have well understood the difference, remember that He endured,

---

* ἀναλογίσασθε (xii. 3).

as you endure, by faith.　He put His trust in God.*
He was faithful to Him Who had constituted Him what
He became through His assumption of flesh and blood.†
He offered prayers and supplications to Him Who was
able to save Him out of death, yet piously committed
Himself to the hands of God.　The gainsaying of men
brought Him to the bloody death of the Cross.　You
also are marshalled in battle array, in the conflict
against the sin of the world.　But the Leader only has
shed His blood—as yet.　Your hour may be drawing
nigh !　Therefore be not weary in striving to reach the
goal !　Faint not in enduring the conflict !　The two
sides of faith are still in the author's thoughts.

It would naturally occur to the readers of the Epistle
to ask why they might not end their difficulties by
shunning the conflict.　Why might they not enter into
fellowship with God without coming into conflict with
men ?　But this cannot be.　Communion with God
requires personal fitness of character, and manifests itself in inward peace.　This fitness, again, is the result
of discipline, and the discipline implies endurance.　" It
is for discipline that ye endure." ‡

The word translated " discipline " suggests the notion

---

* Chap, ii. 13.

| Chap. iii. 2.

‡ εἰς παιδείαν ὑπομένετε (xii. 7, where the verb is indicative, not
imperative).

of a child with his father. But it is noteworthy that the Apostle does not use the word "children" in his illustration, but the word "sons." This was occasioned partly by the fact that the citation from the Book of Proverbs speaks of "sons." But, in addition to this, the author's mind seems to be still lingering with the remembrance of Him Who was Son of God. For discipline is the lot and privilege of all sons. Who is a son whom his father does not discipline? There might have been One. But even He humbled Himself to learn obedience through sufferings. Absolutely every son undergoes discipline.

Furthermore, the fathers of our bodies kept us under discipline, and we not only submitted, but even gave them reverence, though their discipline was not intended to have effect for more than the few days of our pupilage, and though in that short time they were liable to error in their treatment of us. How much more shall we subject ourselves to the discipline of God! He is not only the God of all spirits and of all flesh,* but also the Father of our spirits ; that is, He has created our spirit after His own likeness, and made it capable, through discipline, of partaking in His own holiness, which will be our true and everlasting life. The gardener breaks the hard ground, uproots weeds, lops

---

* Num. xvi. 22,

off branches ; but the consequence of his rough treatment is that the fruit at last hangs on the bough. We are God's tillage.   Our conflict with men and their sin is watched and guided by a Father.   The fruit consists in the calm after the storm, the peace of a good conscience, the silencing of accusers, the putting wicked men to shame, the reverence which righteousness extorts even from enemies.   In the same book from which our author has cited far-reaching instruction, we are told that "when a man's ways please the Lord, He maketh even his enemies to be at peace with him." *

Here, again, the Apostle addresses his readers as members of the Church in its conflict with men.   He tells them that, in doing what is incumbent upon them as a Church towards different classes of men, they secure for themselves individually the discipline of sons and may hope to reap the fruit of that discipline in peace and righteousness.   The Church has a duty to perform towards the weaker brethren, towards the enemy at the gate, and towards the Esaus whose worldliness impures the purity of others.

1. There were among them weaker brethren, the nerves of whose hands and knees were unstrung.   They could neither combat a foe nor run the race.   It was for

---

* Prov. xvi. 7.

the Church to smooth the ruggedness of the road before
its feet, that the lame things * (for so, with something
of contempt, he names the waverers) might not be
turned out of the course by the pressure of the other
runners.   Rather than permit this, let the Church lift
up their drooping hands and sustain their palsied knees
that they may be healed of their lameness.

2. As to enemies and persecutors, it is the duty of the
Church to follow after peace with all men, as much as
in her lies.   Christians may sacrifice almost anything
for peace, but not their own priestly consecration,
without which no man shall see the Lord Jesus at His
appearing.   He will be seen only by those who eagerly
expect Him unto salvation.†

3. The consecration of the Church is maintained
by watchfulness‡ against every tendency to alienation
from the grace of God, to bitterness against God and
the brethren, to sensuality and profane worldliness.
All must watch over themselves and over all the
brethren.   The danger, too, increases if it is neglected.
It begins in withdrawing from§ the Church assemblies,
where the influences of grace are manifested.   It grows
into the poisonous plant of a bitter spirit, which, "like
a root that beareth gall and wormwood," spreads

---

* τὸ χωλόν (xii. 13).   ‡ ἐπισκοποῦντες (xii. 15).
† Chap. ix. 28.   § ὑστερῶν ἀπό.

through "a family or tribe,"* and turns away their
heart from the Lord to go and serve the gods of the
nations. "The many are defiled." The Church as a
whole becomes infected. But bitterness of spirit is not
the only fruit of selfishness. On the same tree
sensuality grows, which God will punish when the
Church cannot detect its presence.†

From the stem of selfishness, which will not brook
the restraints of Church communion, springs, last and
most dangerous of all, the profane, worldly spirit,
which denies and mocks the very idea of consecration.
It is the spirit of Esau, who bartered the right of the
first-born to the promise of the covenant for one mess
of pottage. The author calls attention to the incident,
as it displays Esau's contempt of the promise made to
Abraham and his own father Isaac. His thoughts
never rose above the earth. "What profit shall this
birthright do to me ?"‡ We must distinguish between
the birthright and the blessing. The former carried
with it the great promise given to Abraham with an
oath on Moriah: "In thy seed shall all the nations
of the earth be blessed."§ Possession of it did not
depend on Isaac's fond blessing. It belonged to Esau
by right of birth till he sold it to Jacob. But Isaac's
blessing, which he intended for Esau because he loved

---

* Deut. xxix. 18.   ‡ Gen. xxv. 32.
† Chap. xiii. 4. Cf. Rom. i. 18 sqq.   § Gen. xxii. 18.

him, meant more especially lordship over his brethren.
Esau plainly distinguishes the two things : " Is not he
rightly named Jacob ? For he hath supplanted me
these two times : he took away my birthright, and
behold, now he hath taken away my blessing."* Wher
he found that Jacob had supplanted him a second time
he cried with a great and exceeding bitter cry, and
sought diligently, not the birthright, which was of a
religious nature, but the dew of heaven, and the fatness
of the earth, and plenty of corn and wine, and the
homage of his mother's sons. But he had sold the
greater good and, by doing so, forfeited the lesser.
The Apostle recognises, beyond the subtilty of Jacob
and behind the blessing of Isaac, the Divine retribution.
His selling the birthright was not the merely rash act
of a sorely tempted youth. He continued to despise
the covenant. When he was forty years old, he took
wives of the daughters of the Canaanites. Abraham
had made his servant swear that he would go to the
city of Nahor to take a wife unto Isaac ; and Rebekah,
true to the instinct of faith, was weary of her life
because of the daughters of Heth. But Esau cared for
none of these things. The day on which Jacob took
away the blessing marks the crisis in Esau's life. He
still despised the covenant and sought only worldly

---

* Gen. xxvii. 36.

lordship and plenty. For this profane scorn of the
spiritual promise made to Abraham and Isaac, Esau not
only lost the blessing which he sought, but was himself rejected. The Apostle reminds his readers that
they know it to have been so from Esau's subsequent
history. They would not fail to see in him an example
of the terrible doom described by the Apostle himself
in a previous chapter. Esau was like the earth that
brings forth thorns and thistles and is "rejected."*
The grace of repentance was denied him.†

---

* ἀδόκιμος (vi. 8)　　　　　　　　† Chap. vi. 6.

MOUNT ZION.

" For ye are not come unto *a mount* that might be touched, and that burned with fire, and unto blackness, and darkness, and tempest, and the sound of a trumpet, and the voice of words ; which *voice* they that heard entreated that no word more should be spoken unto them : for they could not endure that which was enjoined, If even a beast touch the mountain, it shall be stoned ; and so fearful was the appearance, *that* Moses said, I exceedingly fear and quake : but ye are come unto Mount Zion, and unto the city of the living God, the heavenly Jerusalem, and to innumerable hosts of angels, to the general assembly and Church of the first-born who are enrolled in heaven, and to God the Judge of all, and to the spirits of just men made perfect, and to Jesus the Mediator of a new covenant, and to the blood of sprinkling that speaketh better than *that of* Abel. See that ye refuse not Him that speaketh. For if they escaped not, when they refused him that warned *them* on earth, much more *shall not* we *escape*, who turn away from Him that *warneth* from heaven : whose voice then shook the earth : but now He hath promised, saying, Yet once more will I make to tremble not the earth only, but also the heaven. And this *word*, Yet once more, signifieth the removing of those things that are shaken, as of things that have been made, that those things which are not shaken may remain. Wherefore, receiving a kingdom that cannot be shaken, let us have grace, whereby we may offer service well-pleasing to God with reverence and awe . for our God is a consuming fire."—HEB. xii. 18--29 (R. V.).

CHAPTER XV.

MOUNT ZION.

MUTUAL oversight is the lesson of the foregoing verses. The author urges his readers to look carefully that no member of the Church withdraws from the grace of God, that no poison of bitterness troubles and defiles the Church as a whole, that sensuality and worldliness are put away. In the paragraph that comes next he still has the idea of Church fellowship in his mind. But his advice to his readers to exercise supervision over one another yields to the still more urgent warning to watch themselves, and especially to shun the most dangerous even of these evils, which is worldliness of spirit. Esau was rejected; see that ye yourselves refuse not Him that speaketh.

That the passage is thus closely connected with what immediately precedes may be admitted. But it must be also connected with the entire argument of the Epistle. It is the final exhortation directly based on the general idea that the new covenant excels the former one. As such it may be compared with the earlier exhorta-

tion, given before the allegory of Melchizedek introduced
the notion that the old covenant had passed away, and
with the warning in the tenth chapter which precedes
the glorious record of faith's heroes from Abel to Jesus.
As early as the second chapter he warns the Hebrew
Christians not to drift away and neglect a salvation
revealed in One Who is greater than the angels, through
whom the Law had been given.   In the later exhortations he adds the notion of the blood of the covenant,
and insists, not merely on the greatness, but also on
the finality, of the revelation.   But in the concluding
passage, which now opens before us, he makes the
daring announcement that all the blessings of the new
covenant have already been fulfilled, and that in perfect
completeness and grandeur.   We *have* come unto
Mount Zion ; we *have* received a kingdom which cannot
be shaken.   The passage must, therefore, be considered
as the practical result of the whole Epistle.

Our author began with the fact of a revelation of
God in a Son.   But a thoughtful reader will not fail
to have observed that this great subject seldom comes to
the front in the course of the argument.   Reading the
Epistle, we seem for a time to forget the thought of a
revelation given in the Son.   Our minds are mastered by
the author's powerful reasoning.   We think of nothing
but the surpassing excellence of the new covenant and
its Mediator.   The greatness of Jesus as High-priest

makes us oblivious of His greatness as the Revealer of God. But this is only the glamour cast over us by a master mind. After all, to know God is the highest glory and perfection of man. Apart from a revelation of God in His Son, all other truths are negative; and their value to us depends on their connection with this self-manifestation of the Father. Religion, theology, priesthood, covenant, atonement, salvation, and the Incarnation itself, do not attain a worthy and final purpose except as means of revealing God. It would be a serious misapprehension to suppose that our author had forgotten this fundamental conception. His aim has been to show that the economy of the new covenant *is* the perfect revelation. God has spoken, not through, but *in*, the Son. The Divine personality, the human nature, the eternal priesthood, the infinite sacrifice, of the Son are the final revelation of God.

In the sublime contrast between Mount Sinai and Mount Zion the two thoughts are brought together. We have had frequent occasion to point out that the central fact of the new covenant is direct communion with God. Access to God is now open to all men in Christ. We are invited to draw near with boldness unto the throne of grace.* Jesus has entered as a Forerunner for us within the veil.† We have boldness

---

* Chap. iv. 16. 　　　　† Chap. vi. 20.

to enter into the holiest by the blood of Jesus.* Yea, we have already actually entered. We are come unto Mount Zion. Death has been annihilated. We are now where Christ is. The writer of our Epistle has advanced beyond the perplexity that, in his hour of loneliness, troubled St. Paul, who was in a strait betwixt two, having a desire to depart and be with Christ, which is far better.† We are come to Jesus, the Mediator of the new covenant. That great city the heavenly Jerusalem has descended out of heaven from God.‡ The angels pass to and fro as ministering spirits. The names of the first-born are registered in heaven, as possessing already the privilege of citizenship. We must not say that the spirits of the righteous have departed from us; let us rather say that we, by being made righteous, have come to them. We stand now before the tribunal of God, the Judge of all. Jesus has fulfilled His promise to come and receive us unto Himself, that where He is, there we may be also.§

All these things are contained in access unto God. The Apostle explains their meaning and unfolds their glory by contrasting them with the revelation of God on Sinai. We might perhaps have expected him to institute a comparison between them and the incidents of the day of atonement, inasmuch as he has described

---

* Chap. x. 19.
† Phil. i. 23.
‡ Rev. xxi. 10.
§ John xiv. 3.

Christ's ascension to the right hand of God as the entering of the High-priest into the true holiest place. But the day of atonement was not a revelation of God. The propitiation required antecedently to a revelation was indeed offered. But, as the propitiation was unreal, the full revelation, to which it was intended to lead, was never given. Nothing is said in the books of Moses concerning the people's state of mind during the time when the high-priest stood in God's presence. The transaction was so purely ceremonial that the people do not seem to have taken any part in it, beyond gathering perhaps around the tabernacle to witness the ingress and egress of the high-priest. Moreover, no words were spoken either by the high-priest before God, or by God to the high-priest or to the people. No prayer was uttered, no revelation vouchsafed. For these reasons the Apostle goes back to the revelation on Sinai, which indeed instituted the rites of the covenant. With the revelation that preceded the sacrifices of the Law he compares the revelation that is founded upon the sacrifice of Christ. This is the fundamental difference between Sinai and Zion. The revelation on Sinai precedes the sacrifices of the tabernacle ; the revelation on Zion follows the sacrifice of the Cross. Under the old covenant the revelation demanded sacrifices ; under the new covenant the sacrifice demands a revelation.

From this essential difference in the nature of the revelations a twofold contrast is apparent in the phenomena of Sinai and Zion. Sinai revealed the terrible side of God's character, Zion the peaceful tenderness of His love. The revelation on Sinai was earthly; that on Zion is spiritual.

There can be no question that the Apostle intends to contrast the terrible appearances on Sinai with the calm serenity of Zion. The very rhythm of his language expresses it. But the key to his description of the one and the other is to be found in the distinction already mentioned. On Sinai the unappeased wrath of God is revealed. Sacrifices are instituted, which, however, when established, evoke no response from the offended majesty of Heaven. Of the holiest place of the old covenant the best thing we can say is that the lightning and thunders of Sinai slumbered therein. The author's beautiful description of the sunny steep of Zion is framed, on the other hand, in accordance with his frequent and emphatic declaration that Christ has entered the true holiest place, having obtained for us eternal redemption. All that the Apostle says concerning Sinai and Zion gathers around the two conceptions of sin and forgiveness.

The Lord spake on Sinai out of the midst of the palpable, enkindled fire, of the cloud, and of the thick darkness, with a great voice. All the people heard the

voice. They saw "that God doth talk with man, and he liveth." They begin to hope. But immediately they bethink them that, if they hear the voice of the Lord any more, they will die. Thus does a guilty conscience contradict itself! Again, the people are invited to come up into the mount when the trumpet shall sound long. Yet, when the voice of the trumpet sounds long and waxes louder and louder, they are charged not to come up unto the Lord, lest He break forth upon them. All this appearance of inconsistency is intended to symbolize that the people's desire to come to God struggled in vain against their sense of guilt, and that God's purpose of revealing Himself to them was contending in vain with the hindrances that arose from their sins. The whole assembly heard the voice of the Lord proclaiming the Ten Commandments. Conscience-smitten, they could not endure to hear more. They gat them into their tents, and Moses alone stood on the mountain with God, to receive at His mouth all the statutes and judgments which they should do and observe in the land which He would give them to possess. The Apostle singles out for remark the command that, if a beast touched the mountain, it should be stoned to death. The people, he says, could not endure this command. Why not this? It connected the terrors of Sinai with man's guilt. According to the Old Testament idea of Divine

retribution, the beasts of the earth fall under the curse
•due to man. When God saw that the wickedness of
man was great in the days of Noah, He said, "I will
destroy both man and beast."·* When, again, He
blessed Noah after the waters were dried up, He said,
"I, behold, I establish My covenant with you and with
every living creature that is with you." † Similarly, the
command to put to death any beast that might haply
touch the mountain revealed to the people that God
was dealing with them as sinners. Moses himself,
the mediator of the covenant, who aspired to behold
the glory of God, feared exceedingly. But his fear
came upon him when he looked and beheld that the
people had sinned against the Lord their God ‡ and
made them a molten calf. His fear was not the
prostration of nervous terror. Remembering, when
he had descended, the awful sights and sounds witnessed on the mountain, he was afraid of the anger
and hot displeasure of God against the people, who
had done wickedly in the sight of the Lord. Almost
every word the Apostle has here written bears closely
upon the moral relation between a guilty people and
the angry God.

If we turn to the other picture, we at once perceive
that the thoughts radiate from the holiest place as from

---

* Gen. vi. 7.　　† Gen. ix. 9, 10.　　‡ Deut. ix. 16, 19.

a centre. The passage is, in fact, an expansion of what
is said in the ninth chapter, that Christ has entered in
once for all into the holiest place, through the greater
and more perfect tabernacle. The holiest has widened
its boundaries. The veil has been removed, so that
the entire sanctuary now forms part of the holy of
holies. It is true that the Apostle begins, in the
passage under consideration, not with the holiest place,
but with Mount Zion. He does so because the immediate contrast is between the two mountains, and he
has already stated that Christ entered through a larger
tabernacle. The holiest place includes, therefore, the
whole mountain of Zion, on which the tabernacle was
erected ; yea, all Jerusalem is within the precincts. If
we extend the range of our survey, we behold the earth
sanctified by the presence of the first-born sons of God,
who are the Church, and of His myriads, the other sons
of God, who also have, not indeed the birthright, but
a blessing, even the joyful multitude of the heavenly
host.* The Apostle describes the angels as keeping
festal holiday, for joy to witness the coming of the first-
born sons. They are the friends of the Bridegroom,

---

* Reading καὶ μυριάσιν, ἀγγέλων πανηγύρει, καὶ ἐκκλησίᾳ πρωτοτόκων
(xii. 22, 23). This disconnected use of μυριάς is amply justified by
Deut. xxxiii. 2, Dan. vii. 10, and Jude 14. Besides, πανήγυρις is
precisely the word to describe the assemblage of angels and distinguish
them from the Church.

who stand and hear Him, and rejoice greatly because of the Bridegroom's voice. If, again, we attempt to soar above this world of trials, we find ourselves at once before the judgment-seat of God. But even here a change has taken place. For we are come to a Judge Who is God of all,* and not merely to a God Who is Judge of all. Thus the promise of the new covenant has been fulfilled, "I will be to them a God."† If in imagination we pass the tribunal and consider the condition of men in the world of spirits, we recognise there the spirits of the righteous dead, and are given to understand that they have already attained the perfection ‡ which they could not have received before the Christian Church had exercised a greater faith than some had found possible to themselves on earth.§ If we ascend still higher, we are in the presence of Jesus Himse'f. But He is on the right hand of the Majesty on high, not simply as Son of God, but as Mediator of the new covenant. His blood is sprinkled on the mercy-seat, and speaks to God, but not for vengeance on those who shed it on the Cross, some of whom possibly were now among the readers of the Apostle's piercing words. What an immeasurable distance between the first man of faith, mentioned in the eleventh chapter, and Jesus, with Whom his list closes ! The very first blood of

---

* κριτῇ θεῳ̣. πάντων.　　　　　‡ τετελειωμένων.
† Chap. viii. 10.　　　　　§ Chap. xi. 40.

man shed to the earth cried from the ground to God for vengeance. The blood of Jesus sprinkled in heaven speaks a better thing. What the better thing is, we are not told. Men may give it a name; but it is addressed to God, and God alone knows its infinite meaning.

From all this we infer that the comparison here made between Sinai and Zion is intended to depict the difference (seen, as it were, in another Bunyan's dream) between a revelation given before Christ offered Himself as a propitiation for sin and the revelation which God gives us of Himself after the sacrifice of Christ has been presented in the true holiest place.

The Apostle's account of Mount Zion is followed by a most incisive warning, introduced with a sudden solemnity, as if the thunder of Sinai itself were heard remote. The passage is beset with difficulties, some of which it would be inconsistent with the design of the present volume to discuss. One question has scarcely been touched upon by the expositors. But it enters into the very pith of the subject. The exhortation which the author addresses to his readers does not at first appear to be based on a correct application of the narrative. For the Israelites at the foot of Sinai are not said to have refused Him that spake to them on the mount. No doubt God, not Moses, is meant; for it was the voice of God that shook the earth. The

people were terrified. They were afraid that the fire
would consume them. But they had understood also
that their God was the living God, and therefore not to
be approached by man. They wished Moses to
intervene, not because they rejected God, but because
they acknowledged the awful greatness of His living
personality. Far from rejecting Him, they said to
Moses, " Speak thou unto us all that the Lord our God
shall speak unto thee ; and we will hear it and do it."*
God Himself commended their words : " They have
well said all that they have spoken." Can we suppose,
therefore, that the Apostle in the present passage
represents them as actually rebelling, and " refusing
Him that spake " ? The word here translated " refuse "†
does not express the notion of rejecting with contempt.
It means " to deprecate," to shrink in fear from a
person. Again, the word " escape," in its reference to
the children of Israel at Sinai, cannot signify " to avoid
being punished," which is its meaning in the second
chapter of this Epistle.‡ The meaning is that they
could not flee from His presence, though Moses
mediated between Him and the people. They could
not escape Him. His word *"found* § them "* when

---

* Deut. v. 27, 28.
† παραιτησάμενοι (xii. 25).
‡ Chap. ii 3
§ " The Bible finds me," said Coleridge.

they cowered in their tents as truly as if they had
climbed with Moses the heights of Sinai.   For the
word of God was then also a living word, and there
was no creature that was not manifest in His sight.
Yet it was right in the people to deprecate, and desire
Moses to speak to them rather than God.   This was
the befitting spirit under the old covenant.   It expresses
very precisely the difference between the bondage of
that covenant and the liberty of the new.   In Christ
only is the veil taken away.   Where the Spirit of the
Lord Jesus is, there is liberty.   But, for this reason,
what was praiseworthy in the people who were kept
at a distance from the bounds placed around Sinai is
unworthy and censurable in those who have come to
Mount Zion.   See, therefore, that ye do not ask Him
that speaketh to withdraw into the thick darkness and
terrible silence.   For us to deprecate is tantamount to
rejection of God.   We are actually turning away from
Him.   But to ignore and shun His presence is now
impossible to us.   The revelation is from heaven.   He
Who brought it descended Himself from above.
Because He is from heaven, the Son of God is a life-
giving Spirit.   He surrounds us, like the ambient air.
The sin of the world is not the only "besetting"
element of our life.   The ever-present, besetting God
woos our spirit.   He speaks.   That His words are
kind and forgiving we know.   For He speaks to us

from heaven, because the blood sprinkled in heaven speaks better before God than the blood of Abel spoke from the ground. The revelation of God to us in His Son preceded, it is true, the entrance of the Son into the holiest place; but it has acquired a new meaning and a new force in virtue of the Son's appearing before God for us. This new force of the revelation is represented by the mission and activity of the Spirit.

The author's thoughts glide almost imperceptibly into another channel. We can refuse Him that speaketh, and turn away from Him in unbelief. But let us beware. It is the final revelation. His voice on Sinai shook the earth. The meaning is not that it terrified the people. The writer has passed from that thought. He now speaks of the effect of God's voice on the material world, the power of revelation over created nature. This is a truth that frequently meets us in Scripture. Revelation is accompanied by miracle. When the Ten Commandments were spoken by the lips of God to the people, " the whole mount quaked greatly." * But the prophet Haggai predicts the glory of the second house in words which recall to our author the trembling of Mount Sinai: " For thus saith the Lord of hosts: Yet once more, it is a little while, and I will shake the heavens, and the earth, and the sea, and

---

* Exod. xix. 18. In his citation of this passage our author forsakes the Septuagint, which has " And all the people were greatly amazed."

the dry land ; and I will shake all nations, and the desir-
able things of all nations shall come, and I will fill this
house with glory, saith the Lord of hosts."*　　It is very
characteristic of the writer of this Epistle to fasten on
a few salient points in the prophet's words.　He seems
to think that Haggai had the scenes that occurred on
Sinai in his mind.　Two expressions connect the
narrative in Exodus with the prophecy.　When God
spoke on Sinai, His voice shook the earth.　Haggai
declares that God will, at some future time, shake the
heaven.　Again, the prophet has used the words "yet
once more."　Therefore, when the greater glory of the
second house will have come to pass, the last shaking
of earth and of heaven will take place.　The inference
is that the word "yet once more" signifieth the
removing of those things that are shaken.　The whole
fabric of nature will perish in its present material form,
and the Apostle connects this universal catastrophe
with the revelation of God in His Son.

Many very excellent expositors think that our author
refers, not to the final dissolution of nature, but to the
abrogation of the Jewish economy.　It is true that the
Epistle has declared the old covenant a thing of the
past.　But there are two considerations that lead us
to adopt the other view of this passage.　In the first

---

* Haggai ii. 6, 7.

place, this Epistle does not describe the abrogation of the old covenant as a violent catastrophe, but rather as the passing away of what had grown old and decayed. In the second place, the coming of the Lord is elsewhere, in writings of that age, spoken of as accompanied by a great convulsion of nature. The two notions go together in the thoughts of the time. "The day of the Lord will come as a thief, in the which the heavens shall pass away with a great noise, and the elements shall be dissolved with fervent heat, and the earth and the works that are therein shall be burned up."*

We connect the words " as things that have been made" with the next clause: "that those things which are not shaken may remain." It is not because they have been made that the earth and the heaven are removed; and their place will not be occupied by uncreated things only, but also by things made. The meaning is that nature will be dissolved when it has answered its purpose, and not till then. Earth and heaven have been made, not for their own sakes, but in order that out of them a new world may be created, which will never be removed or shaken. This new world is the kingdom of which the King-Priest is eternal Monarch.† As we partake in His priesthood, we share also in His kingship. We enter into the

---

* 2 Pet. iii. 10.   † Chap. xii. 28.

holiest place and stand before the mercy-seat, but our absolution is announced and confirmed to us by the Divine summons to sit down with Christ in His throne, as He has sat down with His Father in His throne.*

Let us therefore accept the kingdom.   But beware of your peculiar danger, which is self-righteous pride, worldliness, and the evil heart of unbelief.   Rather let us seek and get that grace from God which will make our royal state a humble service of worshipping priests.†   The grace which the Apostle exhorts his reader to possess is much more than thankfulness. It includes all that Christianity bestows to counteract and vanquish the special dangers of self-righteousness. Such priestly service will be well-pleasing to God. Offer it with pious resignation to His sovereign will, with awe in the presence of His holiness.   For, whilst our God proclaims forgiveness from the mercy-seat as the worshippers stand before it, He is *also* a consuming fire.   Upon the mercy-seat itself rests the Shechinah.

---

* Rev. iii. 21.   † λατρεύωμεν (xii. 29).

SUNDRY EXHORTATIONS.

Let love of the brethren continue. Forget not to shew love unto strangers : for thereby some have entertained angels unawares. Remember them that are in bonds, as bound with them ; them that are evil entreated, as being yourselves also in the body. Let marriage be had in honour among all, and let the bed be undefiled : for fornicators and adulterers God will judge. Be ye free from the love of money ; content with such things as ye have : for Himself hath said, I will in no wise fail thee, neither will I in any wise forsake thee. So that with good courage we say,

> The Lord is my helper ; I will not fear :
> What shall man do unto me?

Remember them that had the rule over you, which spake unto you the word of God ; and considering the issue of their life, imitate their faith. Jesus Christ is the same yesterday and to-day, yea and for ever. Be not carried away by divers and strange teachings : for it is good that the heart be established by grace ; not by meats, wherein they that occupied themselves were not profited. We have an altar, whereof they have no right to eat which serve the tabernacle. For the bodies of those beasts, whose blood is brought into the holy place by the high priest as an offering for sin, are burned without the camp. Wherefore Jesus also, that He might sanctify the people through His own blood, suffered without the gate. Let us therefore go forth unto Him without the camp, bearing His reproach. For we have not here an abiding city, but we seek after the city which is to come. Through Him then let us offer up a sacrifice of praise to God continually, that is, the fruit of lips which make confession to His name. But to do good and to communicate forget not : for with such sacrifices God is well pleased. Obey them that have the rule over you, and submit to them : for they watch in behalf of your souls, as they that shall give account : that they may do this with joy, and not with grief: for this were unprofitable for you.

Pray for us : for we are persuaded that we have a good conscience, desiring to live honestly in all things. And I exhort you the more exceedingly to do this, that I may be restored to you the sooner.

Now the God of peace, who brought again from the dead the great shepherd of the sheep with the blood of the eternal covenant, even our Lord Jesus, make you perfect in every good thing to do His will, working in us that which is well-pleasing in His sight, through Jesus Christ ; to whom be the glory for ever and ever. Amen.

But I exhort you, brethren, bear with the word of exhortation : for I have written unto you in few words. Know ye that our brother Timothy hath been set at liberty ; with whom if he come shortly, I will see you.

Salute all them that have the rule over you, and all the saints. They of Italy salute you.

Grace be with you all. Amen.

CHAPTER XVI.

SUNDRY EXHORTATIONS.

THE condition of the Hebrew Christians was most serious. But one excellence is acknowledged to have belonged to them. It was almost the only ground of hope. They ministered to the saints.* Yet even this grace was in peril. In a previous chapter the writer has exhorted them to call to remembrance the former days, in which they had compassion on them that were in bonds.† But he considers it sufficient, in reference to brotherly love, to urge them to see that it continues.‡ They were in more danger of forgetting to show kindness to their brethren of other Churches, who, in pursuance of the liberty of prophesying accorded in Apostolic times, journeyed from place to place for the purpose of founding new Churches or of imparting spiritual gifts to Churches already established. Besides, it was a time of local persecutions. One Church might be suffering, and its members might take refuge in a sister-Church. Missionaries and persecuted brethren

---

Chap. vi. 10.   † Chap. x. 34.   ‡ Chap. xiii. 1.

would be the strangers to whom the enrolled widows used hospitality, and whose feet they washed.* We can well understand why in that age a bishop would be especially expected to be given to hospitality.† Uhlhorn excellently observes that " the greatness of the age consisted in this very feature : that Christians of all places knew themselves to be fraternally one, and that in this oneness all differences disappeared."‡ In the case of a Church consisting of Hebrews the duty of entertaining strangers, many of them necessarily Greeks, would be peculiarly apt to be forgotten. When a Church wavered in its allegiance to Christianity, the alienation would become still more pronounced.

The constant going and coming of missionary brethren reminds the author of the ministry of angels, who are like the swift breezes, and carry Christ's messages over the face of the earth.§ Sometimes they are as a flame of fire. When they were on their way to destroy the Cities of the Plain, Abraham and Lot entertained them, not knowing that they were heaven-sent ministers of wrath.‖ It would be presumptuous in any man to deny the possibility of angelic visitations in the Christian

---

* 1 Tim. v. 10.
† 1 Tim. iii. 2.
‡ *Christian Charity in the Ancient Church*, English Trans., p. 92.
§ Chap. i. 7.
‖ Gen. xviii. 2 ; xix. 1

Church ; but the Apostle's meaning is not that hospitality ought to be shown to strangers in the hope that angels may be among them. They are to be received unawares ; otherwise the fragrance of the deed is gone. But the fact remains, and has been proved in the experience of many, that kindness to strangers, be they preaching friars, or itinerant exhorters, or persecuted outcasts, brings a rich blessing to children's children. A Syrian builds for himself a hut on the riverside, and offers to carry the wayfarers across on his shoulders. One day a child asks to be taken over. But the light burden becomes every moment heavier. The exhausted bearer asks in astonishment, "Who art thou, child ?" It was Christ, and the Syrian was named the Christ-bearer in remembrance of the event.*

The next exhortation is to purity. It is better not to attempt to connect these exhortations. Their special importance in the case of the Hebrew Christians is reason enough for them. Abstinence from marriage is not commended. Our author is not an Essene. On the contrary, he would discourage it. " Let marriage be held in honour among all classes of men." It is the Divinely appointed remedy against incontinence. But in the married state itself let there be purity. For the

---

* The legend of Christopher is beautifully told by Oosterzee at the beginning of his book on *The Person and Work of the Redeemer,* English Trans. (Ed. 1886).

incontinent, whether in the bonds of wedlock or not, God's direct, providential judgments will overtake.

Then follows a warning against love of money, and the Lord's promise not to fail or forsake Joshua * is appropriated by our author on behalf of his readers. Their covetousness arose from anxiety, which may have been occasioned by their distressing poverty in the days of Claudius.†   That the advice was needed shows the precise character of their threatening apostasy. Worldliness was at the root of their Judaism.   It is still the same.   The self-righteous do not hate money.

Let them imitate the trustfulness of their great leaders in the past, who had not given their time and thoughts to heaping up riches, but had devoted themselves to the work of witnessing and of speaking the word of God.   Let them review with critical eye their manner of life, and observe how it ended.   They all died in faith. Some of them suffered martyrdom, so complete and entirely unworldly was their self-surrender to Jesus Christ !   But Jesus Christ is still the same One.   If He was worthy that Stephen and James should die for His sake, He is worthy of our allegiance too.   Yea, He will be the same for ever.   When the world has passed away, with its fashion and its lust, when the earth and the works that are therein are burned up and dissolved, Jesus Christ abides.   What He was yesterday

---

* Josh. i. 5.   † Acts xi. 28

to His martyr Stephen, that He is to all that follow Him
in earth's to-day, and that He will for ever be when He
shall have appeared unto them who expect Him unto
salvation. The antithesis, it will be seen, is not between
the departed saints and the abiding Christ, but between
the world, which the Hebrew Christians loved too
well, and the Christ Whom the saints of their Church
had loved better than the world and served by faith
unto death.

If Jesus Christ abides, He is our anchorage, and the
exhortation first given near the beginning of the Epistle
once more suggests itself to the Apostle. "Permit
not yourselves to drift and be carried past * the
moorings by divers strange doctrines." The word
"doctrines" is itself emphatic. "Be not borne aside
from the personal, abiding Jesus Christ by propositions,
whether in reference to practice or to belief." What
these "doctrines" were in this particular case we learn
from the next verse. They were the doubtful disputa-
tions about meats. The epithets "divers and strange"
restrict the allusion still more nearly. He speaks not
of the general and familiar injunctions of Jewish
teachers respecting meats, the subject rather contemptuously dismissed by St. Paul in the Epistle to the
Romans: "One man hath faith to eat all things; but
he that is weak eateth herbs." †   Our author could not

---

* $\mu\grave{\eta}\ \pi\alpha\rho\alpha\phi\acute{\epsilon}\rho\epsilon\sigma\theta\epsilon$ (xiii. 9).   † Rom. iv. 13.

have regarded these doctrines as "strange," and he could scarcely have spoken of "strengthening the heart with meats" if he had meant abstinence from meats. A recent English expositor * has pointed out the direction in which we must seek the interpretation of this difficult passage. The Apostle brushes aside the novel teaching of the Essenes, who, without becoming Christians, "had broken away from the sacrificial system" of the Mosaic law and "substituted for it new ordinances of their own, according to which the daily meal became a sacrifice, and the president of the community took the place of the Levitical priest." Such teaching was quite as inconsistent with Judaism as with Christianity. But the writer of this Epistle rejects it for precisely the same reason for which he repudiates Judaism. Both are inconsistent with the perfect separateness of Christ's atonement.

It is well, as St. Paul said, for every man to be fully assured in his own mind.† A doubting conscience enfeebles a man's spiritual vigour for work. The Essenes found a remedy for morbidness in strictness as to meats and minute directions for the employment of time. St. Paul taught that an unhealthy casuistry would be best counteracted by doing all things unto the Lord. "He that eateth eateth unto the Lord, for he giveth God

---

* Kendall : *The Epistle to the Hebrews,* pp. xxv. and 139.
† Rom. xiv. 15.

thanks ; and he that eateth not, unto the Lord he eateth
not, and giveth God thanks.   For none of us liveth to
himself, and none dieth to himself.   For whether we
live, we live unto the Lord ; or whether we die, we
die unto the Lord." *   The author of the Epistle to the
Hebrews considers that it betokens a littleness of soul
to strengthen conscience by regulations as to various
kinds of food.   The noble thing † is that the heart—
that is, the conscience—be stablished by thankfulness,‡
which will produce a strong, placid, courageous, and
healthy moral perception.   The moral code of the New
Testament is direct and simple.   It is entirely free
from all casuistical crotchets and distinctions without
a difference.   Those who busy themselves § about such
matters have never gained anything by it.

Do the Essenes repudiate the altar the sacrifice of
which may not be eaten ?   Do they teach that the only
sacrifice for sin is the daily meal ?   This is a fatal
error.   "We *have*," says the Apostle, "an altar of which
the worshippers are not permitted to eat." ‖   All these
expressions are metaphorical.   By the altar we must
understand the atoning sacrifice of Christ ; by "those

---

* Rom. xiv. 6—8.

† καλόν (xiii. 9).

‡ χάριτι. The author has chosen a more classical word than that
which St. Paul uses.

§ περιπατοῦντες.

‖ Chap. xiii. 10.

who serve the tabernacle " are meant believers in that
sacrifice, prefigured, however, by the priests and
worshippers under the old covenant; and by "eating of
the altar " is meant participation in the sacredness that
pertains to the death and atonement of Christ. The
purpose of the writer is to teach the entire separateness
of Christ's atonement.   It is true that Christians eat
the body and drink the blood of Christ.*   But the
words of our Lord and of St. Paul † refer to the passover,
whereas our author speaks of the sin-offering. In the
former the lamb was eaten;‡ in the latter the carcases
of the beasts whose blood was brought by the worshipper through his representative,§ the high-priest,
into the holiest place on the day of atonement, were
carried forth without the camp and burned in the fire.‖
Both sacrifices, the passover and the sin-offering, were
typical. The former typified our participation in Christ's
death, the latter the separateness of Christ's death.

Many expositors see a reference in the Apostle's
words to the Lord's Table, and some of them infer
from the word "altar" that the Eucharist is a continual
offering of a propitiatory sacrifice to God. It is not too
much to say that this latter doctrine is the precise error
which the Apostle is here combating.

---

* John vi. 51—55.   ‡ Exod. xii.
† I Cor. x. 16.   § διά.
‖ Lev. xvi. 27.

Two other interpretations of these verses have been suggested. Both are, we think, untenable. The one is that we Christians have an altar of which we have a right to eat, but of which the Jewish priests and all who cling to Judaism have no right to eat; and, to prove that they have not, the Apostle mentions the fact that they were not permitted to eat the bodies of the beasts slain as a sin-offering under the old covenant. There are several weighty objections to this view, but the following one will be sufficient. The reference to the sin-offering in the eleventh verse is made in order to show that it was a type of Christ's atoning death. As the bodies of the slain beasts were carried outside the camp and burned, so Christ suffered without the gate. But there is no real resemblance between the two things unless the Apostle intends to teach that the atonement of Christ stands apart and cannot be shared in by any other person, which implies that the tenth verse does not convey the notion that Christians have a right to eat of the altar.

The other interpretation is that we, Christians, have an altar of which we who serve the ideal tabernacle have no right to eat, inasmuch as the sacrifice is spiritual. " Our Christian altar supplies no flesh for carnal food." * But if the reference is to carnal food, the expression

---

* So Rendall, *loc. cit.*

" We have no *right* to eat" is not the appropriate one.
The writer would surely have said, " of which we *cannot*
eat." Besides, this view misses the connection between
the ninth and tenth verses. To say that Christ's death
procured spiritual blessings and that we do not eat His
body after a carnal manner does not affect the question
concerning meats, unless the doctrine concerning meats
includes the notion that they are themselves an atoning
sacrifice. Such was the doctrine of the Essenes. The
argument of the Apostle is good and forcible if it
means that Christ's atonement is Christ's alone. We
share not in its sacredness, though we partake of its
blessings. It resembles the sin-offering on the day of
atonement, as well as the paschal lamb.

But it was not enough that the slain beasts should
be burned without the camp. Their blood also must
be brought into the holiest place. The former rite
signified that the slain beast bore the sin of the people,
the latter that the people themselves were sanctified.
Similarly Jesus suffered without the gate of Jerusalem,
in reproach and ignominy, as the Sin-bearer, and also
entered into the true holiest place, in order to sanctify
His people through His own blood.

We must not press the analogy. The author sees a
quaint but touching resemblance between the burning
of the slain beasts outside the camp and the crucifying
of Jesus on Golgotha outside the city. The point of

resemblance is in the ignominy symbolized in the one and in the other. Here too the writer finds the practical use of what he has said. Though the atonement of the Cross is Christ's, and cannot be shared in by others, the reproach of that atoning death can. The thought leads the Apostle away from the divers strange doctrines of the Essenes, and brings him back to the main idea of the Epistle, which is to induce his readers to hold no more dalliance with Judaism, but to break away from it finally and for ever. " Let us come out," he says. The word recalls St. Paul's exhortation to the Christians of Corinth " to come out from among them, to be separate, and not to touch the unclean thing. For what concord can there be between Christ and Belial, between a believer and an unbeliever, between the sanctuary of God and idols? "* Our author tells the Hebrew Christians that on earth they have nothing better than reproach to expect. Quit, therefore, the camp of Judaism. Live, so to speak, in the desert. (He speaks metaphorically throughout.) You have no abiding city on earth. The fatal mistake of the Jews has been that they have turned what ought to be simply a camp into an abiding city. They have lost the feeling of the pilgrim; they seek not a better country and a city built by God.

---

* 2 Cor. vi. 15 sqq.

Shun ye this worldliness.   Not only regard not your
earthly life as a permanent dwelling in a city, but
leave even the camp; be not only sojourners, but
outcasts.   Share in the reproach of Jesus, and look for
your citizenship in heaven.

Reverting to the teaching of the Essenes, the writer
proceeds : " Through Jesus let us offer a sacrifice of
praise." *   The emphasis must rest on the words
"through Jesus."   The daily meal is not a sacrifice,
except in the sense of being a thanksgiving ; and our
thanksgiving is acceptable to God when it is offered
through Him Whose death is a propitiation.   Even
then lip-worship only is not accepted.   Share the meal
with the poor.   God is pleased with the sacrifices of
doing good to all and contributing † to the necessities
of the saints.

The Apostle next exhorts them to obey their
leaders, and that with yielding submission.   The
atmosphere is certainly different from the democratic
spirit of the Corinthian Church.   Yet it is not improbable that the safety of the Hebrew Christians everywhere from a violent reaction towards Judaism was due
to the wisdom and profounder insight of the leaders.
Our author evidently considers that he has them on his
side.   " They, whatever we may think of the common
herd, are wide awake.   They understand that they

---

* Chap. xiii. 15.   † κοινωνίας.

will have to give an account of their stewardship over you to Christ at His coming. Submit to them, that they may watch over your souls with joy, and not with a grief that finds utterance in frequent sighs.* When they give their account, you will not find that your fretful rebelliousness has profited you aught. The Essenian society gain nothing by absorption of the individual in the community, and you will gain nothing, but quite the reverse, by asserting your individual crotchets to the destruction of the Church." †

He asks his readers to pray for him and Timothy, who has been released from prison. Their prayers are his due. For he believes he has an upright conscience in breaking with Judaism. For the same reason he is confident that their prayers on his behalf will be answered. He and his friends wish in all things to live noble lives. He is the more desirous of having their prayers because of his eagerness to be "restored" ‡ to them. He means much more than to return to them. He wishes to be " restored," or " refitted." Their prayers will put an end to the perturbation of his mind, and bring back the happiness of their first love.

He, too, prays for them. His prayer is that God may furnish them with every gift of grace to do His will, and His will is their consecration,§ through the

---

* στενάζοντες (xiii. 17).   ‡ ἀποκατασταθῶ (xiii. 18).
† ἀλυσιτελές. Comp. ver 9.   § Chap. x. 10.

offering of the body of Jesus Christ once. God will
answer his prayer and provide in them that which is
pleasing in His sight through Jesus Christ. For He
has not left His Church without a Shepherd, though
it is in the wilderness. He has brought up from
the dead, and restored out of the ignominious death
without the gate, our Lord Jesus Christ, the great
Shepherd, Who is ever with them, whatever may become
of the undershepherds. That He has been raised
from the dead is certain. For, when He was crucified
in ignominy without the gate, His blood was at the
same time offered in the true holiest place. That blood
has ratified the new and final covenant between God
and His people. It was through His own blood of
this eternal covenant that He was raised from the dead,
and it is in virtue of the same blood and of the same
covenant that He is now the Shepherd of His Church.

Here, again, we must not draw too broad a distinction
between the resurrection of Christ and His ascension
to heaven. On the one hand, we must not say that by
the words " bringing up from the dead" the Apostle
means the ascension ; on the other hand, the words
do not exclude the ascension. The resurrection and
the ascension coalesce in the notion of Christ being
living. The only distinction present, we think, to
the writer's mind was that between the shame of
Christ's death without the camp and the offering of

His blood by the living Christ in the holiest place. He Who died on the Cross through that death liveth evermore. He lives to be the Shepherd of His people. Therefore to Him must be ascribed the glory for ever and ever.

The Apostle once more begs his readers to bear with the word of exhortation. Let them remember that he has written briefly in order to spare them. He might have said more, but he has refrained.

He hopes to bring Timothy with him, unless his friend tarries long. In that case he will come alone, so great is his anxiety to see them.

He sends his greetings to all the saints, but mentions the leaders. Brethren who have come from Italy are with him. They may have been exiles or fugitives who had sought safety during the first great persecution of the Church in the days of Nero. They too send greetings.

He closes with the Apostolic benediction. For, whoever he was, he was truly an Apostolic man.

INDEX.

0203	Dolman, Dirk H.	The Tabernacle	19.75
0603	Lang, John M.	Studies in the Book of Judges	17.75
0701	Cox, S. & Fuller, T.	The Book of Ruth	14.75
0902	Deane, W. J. & Kirk, T.	Studies in the First Book of Samuel	19.00
1301	Kirk, T. & Rawlinson, G.	Studies in the Books of Kings	20.75
2102	Wardlaw, Ralph	Exposition of Ecclesiastes	16.25
4603	Jones, John Daniel	Exposition of First Corinthians 13	9.50
4902	Pattison, R. & Moule, H.	Exposition of Ephesians: Lessons in Grace and Godliness	14.75
5104	Daille, Jean	Exposition of Colossians	24.95
5803	Edwards, Thomas C.	The Epistle to the Hebrews	13.00
5903	Stier, Rudolf E.	Commentary on the Epistle of James	10.25
6202	Morgan, J. & Cox, S.	The Epistles of John	22.95
7000	Tatford, Frederick Albert	The Minor Prophets(3 vol.)	44.95
7107	Cox, S. & Drysdale, A. H.	The Epistle to Philemon	9.25
8403	Jones, John Daniel	The Apostles of Christ	10.00
8404	Krummacher, Frederick W.	David, King of Israel	20.50
8405	MacDuff, John Ross	Elijah, the Prophet of Fire	13.75
8406	MacDuff, John Ross	The Footsteps of St. Peter	24.25
8801	Lidgett, John Scott	The Biblical Doctrine of the Atonement	19.50
8802	Laidlaw, John	The Biblical Doctrine of Man	14.00
9513	Innes, A. T. & Powell, F. J.	The Trial of Christ	10.75
9514	Gloag, P. J. & Delitzsch, F.	The Messiahship of Christ	23.50
9515	Blaikie, W. G. & Law, R.	The Inner Life of Christ	17.25
9806	Ironside, H. A. & Ottman, F.	Studies in Biblical Eschatology	16.00

TITLES CURRENTLY AVAILABLE

0101	Delitzsch, Franz	A New Commentary on Genesis (2 vol.)	30.50
0102	Blaikie, W. G.	Heroes of Israel	19.50
0103	Bush, George	Genesis (2 vol.)	29.95
0201	Murphy, James G.	Commentary on the Book of Exodus	12.75
0202	Bush, George	Exodus	22.50
0301	Kellogg, Samuel H.	The Book of Leviticus	21.00
0302	Bush, George	Leviticus	10.50
0401	Bush, George	Numbers	17.75
0501	Cumming, John	The Book of Deuteronomy	16.00
0602	Bush, George	Joshua & Judges (2 vol. in 1)	17.95
1101	Farrar, F. W.	The First Book of Kings	19.00
1201	Farrar, F. W.	The Second Book of Kings	19.00
1701	Raleigh, Alexander	The Book of Esther	9.75
1802	Green, William H.	The Argument of the Book of Job Unfolded	13.50
1901	Dickson, David	A Commentary on the Psalms (2 vol.)	32.50
1902	MacLaren, Alexander	The Psalms (3 vol.)	45.00
2001	Wardlaw, Ralph	Book of Proverbs (3 vol.)	45.00
2101	MacDonald, James M.	The Book of Ecclesiastes	15.50
2201	Durham, James	An Exposition on the Song of Solomon	17.25
2301	Kelly, William	An Exposition of the Book of Isaiah	15.25
2302	Alexander, Joseph	Isaiah (2 vol.)	29.95
2401	Orelli, Hans C. von	The Prophecies of Jeremiah	15.25
2601	Fairbairn, Patrick	An Exposition of Ezekiel	18.50
2701	Pusey, Edward B.	Daniel the Prophet	19.50
2702	Tatford, Frederick Albert	Daniel and His Prophecy	9.25
3001	Cripps, Richard S.	A Commentary on the Book of Amos	13.50
3201	Burn, Samuel C.	The Prophet Jonah	11.25
3801	Wright, Charles H. H.	Zechariah and His Prophecies	24.95
4001	Morison, James	The Gospel According to Matthew	24.95
4101	Alexander, Joseph	Commentary on the Gospel of Mark	16.75

TITLES CURRENTLY AVAILABLE